HARVARD HISTORICAL MONOGRAPHS
I

PUBLISHED UNDER THE DIRECTION OF THE DEPARTMENT
OF HISTORY FROM THE INCOME OF

THE ROBERT LOUIS STROOCK FUND

LONDON : HUMPHREY MILFORD
OXFORD UNIVERSITY PRESS

Athenian Tribal Cycles in the Hellenistic Age

BY

WILLIAM SCOTT FERGUSON

Cambridge
HARVARD UNIVERSITY PRESS
MCMXXXII

COPYRIGHT, 1932
BY THE PRESIDENT AND FELLOWS OF HARVARD COLLEGE

PRINTED AT THE HARVARD UNIVERSITY PRESS
CAMBRIDGE, MASS., U. S. A.

IN MEMORY

OF

ROBERT LOUIS STROOCK

CONTENTS

ROBERT LOUIS STROOCK xi
PROLOGUE 3

PART I
THE THIRD CENTURY B.C.

I. NEW LIGHT ON EKPHANTOS AND DIOMEDON . . . 11
II. ALTERNATE PRIESTLY CYCLES OF ASKLEPIOS . . . 19
III. THE RELATION OF PRIESTLY TRIBAL CYCLES TO INVENTORIES 39
IV. TRIBAL CYCLES WITH ALLOTTED ORDER OF *PHYLAE* 48
V. STABILITY OF PRIESTLY CYCLES OF ASKLEPIOS . . 65
VI. PHILIPPOS, KIMON, XENOPHON, PEITHIDEMOS 66
VII. TRIBAL CYCLES AND ARCHONS DURING THE DARKEST AGE 75
VIII. TRIBAL CYCLES, ARCHONS, AND PRIESTS BETWEEN 230/29 AND 201/0 B.C. 90
IX. THE EPHEBE LISTS OF THE THIRD CENTURY B.C. . 102
X. THE ARCHON POLYEUKTOS AND THE AETOLIAN SOTERIA 107

PART II
THE SECOND CENTURY B.C. AND AFTER

XI. THE CRISIS OF 201/0 B.C. 139
XII. THE SECRETARY-CYCLE WITH ALLOTTED ORDER OF *PHYLAE*, 157/6–146/5 B.C. 145
XIII. CONSTITUTIONAL CRISES OF 103–88 B.C. 147
XIV. TRIBAL CYCLES OF ATHENIAN PRIESTS AT DELOS . 155
XV. THE CHANGE IN THE PRIESTLY CYCLE OF ASKLEPIOS IN 157 B.C. 171
EPILOGUE 176
INDEX 185

LIST OF TABLES

I. Military officials, so far as they are datable, between 261/0 and 230/29 B.C. 14

II. Archons, prytany-secretaries, and datable priests of Asklepios between 307/6 and 48/7 B.C. 22

III. *Archontes* (designated by numbers of their *phylae*) between 230/29 and 213/2 B.C., 103/2 and 96/5 B.C., and in isolated years after 91 B.C. 50

IV. Archons listed in IG^2 II 1706 (230/29–213/2 B.C.) . . 97

V. Ephebe officials between 269/8 and 185/4 B.C. 104

VI. Delian priests (*demotika* only) between 166/5 and 92/1 B.C. 156

VII. Priests of Aphrodite Hagne between 121/0 and 97/6 B.C. 163

VIII. Tribal distribution of Delian priesthoods rotating in the official order, 166/5–91 B.C. 170

ROBERT LOUIS STROOCK
A.B. (1927), A.M. (1928)

THE young scholar, to perpetuate whose memory the Robert Louis Stroock Fund was created, possessed qualities of mind and character worthy of remembrance. He was born in New York City on July 13th, 1905. His father, Sol M. Stroock, a college man by education and a lawyer by profession, taught him by his own example the attractiveness of a student's life. His mother, Hilda Weil Stroock, also a college graduate, was fortunate in being able to share her son's intellectual aspirations. Robert had the inestimable advantage of a boyhood free from material cares and bound by a liberalizing tradition.

After attending the Alcuin School, he prepared for college at the Horace Mann School for Boys in New York City, and entered Harvard in September, 1923. His was essentially a loyal nature: he was loyal to his School, his College, his teachers, his friends, and, above all, to his home. It was characteristic that while at Harvard he subtracted generously from his allowance to help promising boys through school, and that he did this so quietly that the fact became known to his parents only after his death. His college days were busy, his diversions (including chess) non-athletic, his scholarly interests at first, as was proper, diversified, later, with lasting benefit, focused on the history and literature of England. He graduated in 1927 in the first tenth of his class with Honors in his chosen field. His instructors were impressed by his mental alertness, his youthful enthusiasm, his charm of manner, his independence of thought untinctured with self-assertion, and his fearlessness of hard work. He did not make friends easily or widely, but those he made he kept and to them he opened his mind freely. They knew him as a thinker, eagerly exploring new ideas and testing their reactions on himself; as an insatiate reader, unabashed before the masters yet haling the moderns before their tribunal; as a dreamer, with a spirit greatly but not unhealthily introspective.

Robert Stroock was one of the group, deplorably small in America, of ambitious and capable students who enter upon graduate studies without having needed to receive financial assistance while in college. His choice of calling was free, and he exercised it without hesitation. He was not irresponsive to the adventure of action which attracts so strongly young men of ample means in America; but the adventure of thought attracted him yet more strongly. As an undergraduate he had quickened his historical imagination, and strengthened his command of foreign languages, by travel in Europe; so that, on entering the Harvard Graduate School in the autumn of 1927, he knew that he was to be an historian. But he had not yet determined his special field of history. His first year of graduate work was experimental: he tried out various historical subjects as yet unexplored by him, and various new instructors. His final selection of specialty was dictated mainly by private predilection. Denied the chance to study Greek in school by exigencies of curriculum, he studied it out of school under the guidance of a private teacher; and his decision to seek his spiritual salvation in the quest for knowledge and understanding of ancient Greece was long premeditated. It led him in 1928–29 to the American School of Classical Studies at Athens, and it was confirmed by his experience there.

His year in Greece was joyous and fruitful. He entered whole-heartedly into all the activities of the School, and he prepared a paper on the *kalos*-names on Athenian vases in which he broke new ground. Returning to Harvard in the autumn of 1929, he threw himself with ardor into the investigation of problems in Greek History with Ferguson, Greek Archaeology with Chase, and Greek Religion with Nock. He was at the height of his powers. In the spring of 1930 he was tempted by an opportunity to teach his subject in Smith College, but, though he looked forward with pleasure to the prospect of imparting knowledge, he had the wisdom to desire to make sure that he had it first. His studies had drawn him into an examination of the inventories of the Treasurers of Athena; and he was hard at work on the published texts preparatory to studying the originals in the Epigraphical Museum at Athens when in April, 1930, he was stricken with a malignant infection. Engrossed though he was with the financial problems of Pericles, and tantalized by the glimpses of the interests, thinking, and aspirations of the Athenians which the Attic inscriptions offer to their votaries, he sought, as always, to relate his daily tasks to his vision, profoundly mystical, of his life as a whole. His *Letters* (privately printed at the Southworth Press, Portland, Maine, in 1932) show that his imagination had been caught by what Wilamowitz terms eine ewige Wahrheit: τἄλλα πάντα κοινὰ εἶναι τῶν ἀνθρώπων, τὴν δ' ἐπὶ τὸν οὐρανὸν ἀνθρώπους φέρουσαν ὁδὸν Ἀθηναίους εἰδέναι μόνους. "To transport Athens to America," that is how he worded his final dream.

He died in his parents' home in New York City on December 30th, 1930. *Sunt lacrimae rerum.*

ABBREVIATIONS

AJA	American Journal of Archaeology
AJP	American Journal of Philology
BCH	Bulletin de correspondance hellénique
CAH	Cambridge Ancient History
Dinsmoor ..	The Archons of Athens in the Hellenistic Age, Cambridge, Mass., 1931
FGH	Jacoby, Die Fragmente der griechischen Historiker
GDI	Collitz-Bechtel-Hoffmann, Sammlung der griechischen Dialekt-Inschriften
GGA	Goettingische Gelehrte Anzeigen
JHS	Journal of Hellenic Studies
PW	Real-Encyclopaedie der classischen Altertums-Wissenschaft, hrsg. von Wissowa-Kroll
REA	Revue des études anciennes
REG	Revue des études grecques
Roussel, *Délos*	Délos, Colonie Athènienne, Paris, 1916
SEG	Supplementum Epigraphicum Graecum

My own writings (*Athenian Secretaries*, Cornell Studies in Classical Philology, VII, 1898; *Athenian Archons*, ibid., X, 1899; *Priests of Asklepios*, Univ. of Calif. Public. Class. Phil., I, 1907, pp. 131 ff.; *Hell. Ath.* = *Hellenistic Athens*, London, 1911; *Treasurers of Athena*, Cambridge, Mass., 1932) are cited by title alone.

PROLOGUE

MY FRIEND Dinsmoor has done me the honor — the very great honor — of dedicating to me his book on *The Archons of Athens in the Hellenistic Age*; and I am both gratified by the homage of the act and proud to have my name associated thus with so remarkable a work. The materials for the study of the chronology of Athens between the "tyranny" of Lachares and the epoch of Augustus are assembled, sifted, and combined in this book as nowhere else; and for the first time a sustained effort has been made to determine the calendar actually used by the Athenians during the 323 years between the epoch-making reform of Meton in 432 B.C. and the completion of his seventeenth cycle in 109 B.C. Text, tables, and indices are models of exposition. Taken together, they furnish the interested inquirer with all the relevant facts and arguments available at the date of publication. Question after question which distracted previous investigators has been set aright and answered. The pros and cons of ancient controversies are stated firmly and fairly. Even on points in regard to which I shall take issue with the distinguished student of architecture whom the happy discovery of a notable inscription and the fascination (which I have long experienced) of a perplexing puzzle have drawn into the subject of Athenian chronology, I have seldom found it possible to improve his statements of the case. I have noted, I believe, some essential new facts and combinations; but in evaluating them I have had the inestimable advantage of finding the data with which they are to be integrated tested and tabulated with discrimination and impartiality. I should like thus initially to record my obligations to Dinsmoor, since it happens, unavoidably, that when I mention his name in the following pages, it is oftener than not to register dissent. Were I to discuss the particulars on which he has left nothing further to be said, or in which I agree with him, frequently unlearning what I myself have taught, I should be guilty, oftentimes, of vain repetitions and should have to recast the whole plan of my monograph. Its subject, I should like to emphasize, is the *Tribal Cycles*, not the *Archons*, of Athens in the Hellenistic Age. For all considerations bearing on the dating of particular archons, apart from those indispensable for the construction of cycles, I should like to refer the reader, once for all, to Dinsmoor's superb quarto.[1]

Appreciating the extent of my interest in the investigations he was pursuing, Dinsmoor took me into his confidence at an early stage, and we exchanged opinions on many of the salient points involved. His methods of work are, I am firmly convinced, sound; and he has

[1] I am indebted to Professor B. D. Meritt for letting me insert in Table II, in advance of his publication in future numbers of *Hesperia*, the names of some new secretaries and archons found in the course of the recent excavations of the American School in the Athenian agora: namely, those of the years 247/6?, 219/8 204/3, 172/0, and 125/4 B.C. Cf. also *below*, pp. 98, 104 ff. Mr. Sterling Dow, Fellow of Harvard University in the American School, has given me invaluable help in determining anew the readings of texts in Athens and Delphi. I have had further aid from Professor Dinsmoor. My colleagues, Professors A. D. Nock and G. H. Chase, have saved me from various errors which cropped up in their reading of my manuscript. To all these gentlemen I wish to express my appreciation and thanks.

used them with a detachment of which, in view of earlier commitments, I am probably incapable. I have long disbelieved in the existence of an invariable sequence of ordinary and intercalary months in the Metonic Cycle (*Class. Phil.*, 1908, pp. 386 ff.), and am gratified that Dinsmoor (see especially pp. 370 ff.) has now proved that my scepticism was justified. We have henceforth to reckon in Athens with a flexible calendar; yet it is clear that the Athenians were not completely free to add an intercalary month in any year. They avoided a succession of two intercalary and three ordinary years, as was natural, and they intercalated only seven months in each cycle of nineteen years. They thus kept the beginning of their year not too far distant from the summer solstice and saw to it that at the end of each Metonic Cycle the initial relation of lunar and solar periods was approximately reëstablished. Accordingly, the calendar cycle becomes of secondary importance in the dating of Athenian archons[1] and the priority of the Tribal Cycles for this purpose is vindicated.

[1] The sequence of three ordinary years in 306/5–304/3 B.C. (Dinsmoor, pp. 375 ff.) resulted from the decision of the Athenians to make 307/6 B.C. (instead of 306/5) an intercalary year, their object being to augment the length of the year so that when the prytanies were increased by the organization of Antigonis and Demetrias, the term of service of the tribes which served subsequently should not be unduly short. Dinsmoor (pp. 377 ff.) has helped us greatly to understand how this was done. Similarly, in the first Metonic Cycle the year 426/5 B.C. was made intercalary instead of 425/4 (cf. Meritt, *The Athenian Calendar*, pp. 89 ff.; Dinsmoor, pp. 322, 333). From these instances we see that irregularities might be corrected at the first opportunity and not solely at the end of the cycle. I am inclined to agree with Beloch (*Griech. Gesch.*, IV 2, p. 21) that 318/7 B.C. was an ordinary year in which the lengths of the prytanies were disturbed. It was the first year of the democratic restoration and at the same time the year of the

Dinsmoor has discovered a new aid to chronological determinations. He has observed that the limits of Tribal Cycles were significant for the beginning and ending of inventories, lists of magistrates, and other like records. In what follows I have tested this observation and found it valid. It yields results of considerable importance.

In one particular I feel obliged to modify the conception of Tribal Cycles accepted hitherto by other scholars as well as by Dinsmoor. Athens knew *two* ways of effecting a rotation of offices "by tribes" (κατὰ φυλάς): it used the fixed sequence of the tribes; and it determined by annual sortition their succession within the cycle. Hence in instances where the fixed sequence was abandoned we have to consider whether the allotted sequence was substituted for it. We cannot assume without investigation that the Tribal Cycles were broken.

Scientific results are conditioned not only by methods of research but also by the materials to which they are applied; and Dinsmoor is too well aware of the dearth of well-established facts in this field of inquiry to feel surprised that, while agreeing with his conclusions on

---

inauguration of the government of Demetrius of Phaleron. It then becomes unnecessary to postulate, with Dinsmoor, another series of three ordinary years in the seventh Metonic Cycle (318/7–300/299 B.C.). Of the nine cycles which can be reconstructed (the sixth, seventh, eighth, ninth, tenth, eleventh, twelfth, fourteenth, and sixteenth) only the eighth and the tenth, and the fourteenth and sixteenth can have been alike. Alternate restorations, which are possible, would make them all different. Since, however, as my colleague Professor O. D. Kellogg informed me, there are 113 distinct ways of constructing cycles which meet the requirements stated in the text, this diversity is not surprising.

certain major questions, I felt obliged to retain an open mind in regard to others. To be specific. In the all-important matter of the secretary-cycles I have little doubt that Dinsmoor is right in his reconstruction between 295/4 and 263/2 B.C. and between 145/4 B.C. and the capture of Athens by Sulla, but in regard to his scheme for the intervening period or periods I have felt constrained hitherto to suspend judgment. Excepting Thrasyphon (221/0 B.C.) and Archon and Epikrates (147/5 B.C.), there is not a single archon in this entire interval, and consequently not a single secretary, whose precise year is incapable of being moved, and with him the secretary-cycles, by one twelve months or more — ordinarily more; for we shall have, I think, to grant to Dinsmoor the *possibility* that Xenokles, hitherto assigned, on what seemed adequate grounds, to 168/7 B.C., may have held office in 169/8 B.C. instead.

PART I
THE THIRD CENTURY B.C.

PART I

THE THIRD CENTURY B.C.

I. New Light on Ekphantos and Diomedon

THE points which have led me to hesitate have been essentially three: the probability that Xenokles belongs in 168/7 B.C.;[1] the probability that the deme of

---

[1] According to Apollodoros (Jacoby, *FGH*, II B, 244, 47) "it was after the capture of Perseus, in the archonship of Xenokles, that Agamestor, son of Polyxenos, of Arcadia ended his life." The battle of Pydna fell in the consulship of L. Aemilius and C. Licinius, 168 B.C. More precisely it is reported to have been fought on the day after the eclipse of the moon which occurred during the evening of June 21st, 168 B.C. (*Livy*, XLIV, 37, 5 f.; Plut., *Aem.*, 17, 3 ff.; Niese, *Gesch. d. griech. u. maked. Staaten*, III, p. 161, n. 4. Polybius (XXIX, 16) does not necessarily bring the eclipse into close connection with Pydna). If this is correct, the battle took place near the end of the archon-year 169/8 B.C. But there is a variant report (Meyer, *Sitz. Ber. Akad.*, 1909, p. 782, n. 1) which dates the battle "in the latter end of summer" (θέρους γὰρ ἦν ὥρα φθίνοντος, Plut., *Aem.*, 16, 5; cf. *post circumactum solstitium*, i.e. after June 26th, *Livy*, XLIV, 36, 1). This later date is commonly thought to be an error arising from the equation of June 22d with the 4th of September in the Roman calendar (*pridie nonas Septembres*, *Livy*, XLIV, 37, 8; cf. XLV, 1, 6 and 11). Beloch, on the other hand, roundly declares that the connection of Pydna with the eclipse of June 21st is a legend (*Griech. Gesch.*, IV 2, p. 114; cf. Jacoby, *FGH*, II BD, p. 855), and dates the battle later in the year, in August–September, perhaps.

It is hard to reconcile the later date with the account given by Plutarch (*Aem.*, 36, 3) of Aemilius' actions before the battle. He makes Aemilius say, "In one day I crossed the Ionian Sea from Brundisium and put in at Corcyra; thence, in five days, I came to Delphi and sacrificed to the god; and again, in other five days, I took command of the forces in Macedonia, and after the usual lustration and review of them I proceeded at once to action, and in other fifteen days brought the war to the most glorious issue" (Trans. by Perrin, *Loeb Classics*). In view of such great expedition after leaving Rome, we

the secretary for Thrasyphon's year (Paiania) belongs to the tribe Pandionis and not to Antigonis;[1] and the

may well ask why Aemilius deferred his departure from the city till near the first of August. But it is almost equally difficult to reconcile the early date with the account given by Livy and Plutarch of the events which followed the battle. After describing the meeting at Pella between Perseus, captured on Samothrace not long before, and Aemilius, Livy (XLV, 9, 1; cf. Plut., *Aem.*, 28, 1) tells us that the Roman "army was then (*deinde*) sent into winter quarters." Can we assume that some three months intervened between the battle of Pydna and the capture of Perseus? Is it easier to believe that the army went into winter quarters in midsummer? Livy is at least consistent with himself. While he makes the news of Pydna reach Rome in thirteen days, he states that the letters announcing the capture of Perseus were brought to the capital later than the arrival there of the ambassadors dispatched by Antiochos and Ptolemy after the settlement of the Egyptian question by Popilius (XLV, 13, 9). Yet we do not need the report of Polybius (XXIX, 27, 12; cf. XXX, 16) to know that Antiochos had heard of the defeat of Perseus when he yielded to Roman intimidation.

This being the state of the derivative sources, it seems logical to fall back upon Polybius. He tells us (III, 1, 9) that 53 years lie between the beginning of his work in Ol. 140, 1 (220/19 B.C.) and "the overthrow of the monarchy in Macedonia." Clearly he dated the end of Perseus' reign in 168/7 B.C. Since he expressly mentions the 140th Olympiad as the starting point for this computation, (cf. I, 3, 1) Dinsmoor's construction (p. 509) is inadmissible. The dates of Porphyrios are too uncertain to warrant us in putting any reliance on the year (Ol. 152, 4, 169/8 B.C.) assigned by him to the capture of Perseus (Jacoby, *FGH*, II BD, p. 855).

The probabilities seem to me clearly to favor dating the death of Agamestor and the archonship of Xenokles in 168/7 B.C. There is at most a bare possibility that they belong in 169/8.

[1] The only *Paianieis* known to have belonged to Antigonis are the three ephebes listed in *IG*² II 478 (305/4 B.C.). All other members of this deme whose *phyle* is determinable between 307/6 and 200 B.C. belonged to Pandionis (*IG*² II 1152?; 1159, 1160, 303/2 B.C.; 653, 654, 655, 287/6 B.C.; 665, 268/7 B.C.; 766, Philoneos archon, 242/1? B.C.; 787, Kimon archon, 237/6 B.C.; 792, *ca.* 230 B.C.; 1706, col. i, 6, Heliodoros archon, 229/8 B.C.; 1706, col. i, 27, Theophilos archon, 227/6 B.C.). As Bates (*The Five Post-Kleisthenean Tribes*, Cornell Studies, VIII, p. 12) pointed out, it was Upper Paiania that was transferred to Antigonis. The prytany-lists, *IG*² II 1740,

improbability that Heliodoros precedes 229/8 B.C.[1] To these a fourth has now been added: the improbability, not to say the impossibility, that Ekphantos can have preceded 237/6 B.C. Dinsmoor is obliged by his scheme of cycles to date Ekphantos in 239/8 B.C. It then follows from combining the data contained in the inscription from Rhamnus recently published by Stavropoullos ('Ελληνικά, III, pp. 153 ff.; cf. Kougeas, *idem*, pp. 281 ff.) and republished by Roussel (*BCH*, 1930, pp. 268 ff.) with the data contained in IG^2 II 1299 (see Table I) that Apollonios of Thria was appointed *strategos* by Demetrius in 242/1 B.C. at the latest — a sheer impossibility. The force of this argument would be broken if we could concede to Dinsmoor (letter) that in one year (the archonship of Kimon or Lysias) there were two *strategi* in the Eleusinian district, Apollonios and Aristophanes of Leukonoe; but, even with this concession, which no one would claim unless he were obliged to date Ekphantos in 239/8 B.C., the difficulty remains that Apollonios would have entered upon his generalship at Rhamnus in 241 B.C., before the earliest possible date for the accession of Demetrius to the throne, unless he were an extraordinary appointee of the Macedonian king for the last few months of 241/0 B.C. These are serious difficulties. They fall to the ground when we retain the date (236/5 B.C.) given to Ekphantos on the basis of the secretary-cycle hitherto

---

1748, show that Upper Paiania had only a small fraction of the population of Lower Paiania which remained in Pandionis (cf. IG^2 II 1700, 1751, 1753). Consequently the probabilities favor strongly the common opinion that the secretary for Thrasyphon's year belonged to the latter *phyle*.

[1] See *below*, pp. 94 f.

TABLE I

Year	Archon	Eleusis	Office	Paralia	Office	Piraeus
261/0	Sosistratos?					Hierokles?
260/9	Philostratos	Thukritos	Hipparch	Kallisthenes	Phylarch	
259/8	Phanostratos			Kallisthenes	Strategos	
258/7	Pheidostratos			Kallisthenes	Strategos	
257/6	Antimachos	Demetrios	Hipparch and Strategos	Kallisthenes	Hipparch	
256/5	Kleomachos			Thukritos?	Strategos	
255/4	Polyeuktos			Thukritos	Strategos	
254/3	Hieron					Herakleitos
253/2	Diomedon					
252/1	Diogeiton					
251/0	Theophemos					
250/9	Kydenor			Apollodoros?	Strategos	
249/8	Eurykleides					
248/7	Lysiades	Demetrios?	Strategos			
247/6	Olbios?					
246/5	Kallimedes			Thukritos	Strategos	
245/4	Lysitheides?					

[14]

244/3	Thersilochos			
243/2	Thymochares?			
242/1	Philoneos?			
241/0				
240/9	Athenodoros			
239/8	Charikles			
238/7	Lysias	Apollonios	Strategos	Thukritos Strategos
237/6	Kimon	Aristophanes	Strategos	
236/5	Ekphantos	Aristophanes	Strategos	Apollonios* Strategos
235/4	Lysanias			Philokedes Strategos
234/3				
233/2	Jason?			Diogenes
232/1				
231/0				
230/9				

* Appointed by King Demetrius. The son of Apollonios, Dikaiarchos, commandant at Eretria in Ekphantos' archonship (236/5 B.C.), had been an officer (*hegemon?*) under his father both at Rhamnus and Eleusis (Panakton). The Eleusinian district included three fortresses, Eleusis, Panakton, and Phyle; the Paralian two, Rhamnus and Sunion. Salamis belonged to the Piraeic district.

in vogue, as is made clear by Table I (pp. 14–15), in which are listed in chronological order (so far as this is ascertainable) the military officials holding commands in the several districts into which Attica was divided during the Macedonian period.

The reasons actuating Dinsmoor in supplanting the Tribal Cycles thitherto current (which for convenience of citing I shall often call mine, though many scholars, notably Kirchner, have helped to establish them) by cycles of his own are essentially two: first Diomedon, and secondly his construction of the Tribal Cycles of the priests of Asklepios. In regard to Diomedon I have something further to add. The initial letter of the *demotikon* of the secretary in IG^2 II 791 has been read as an alpha, a lambda, and a delta. The stone has been reëxamined again and again on my behalf by Mr. Sterling Dow. On one point his findings are definite: "the last letter of line four, read formerly as lambda, has a bar near the base. This is perfectly clear on the squeeze." Both the squeeze and the photograph sent me by Mr. Dow show the cross-bar unmistakably. The only question is how there can ever have been any doubt about it. The explanation given by Mr. Dow is that, as he himself experienced, the cross-bar, which is much less deep than the other two strokes of the letter, is not perceptible in the light in which the stone lies in the Epigraphical Museum. "At each of two inspections," he affirms, "the last letter of line four seemed certainly to be a lambda. The squeeze showed the cross-bar. It is totally invisible as the stone lies, could barely be felt, but appeared when charcoal was used." It must be remembered that Köhler made out the cross-bar and that Johnson (*AJP*, 1913, p. 386; *Class. Phil.*, 1914, p. 436) read it on his squeeze. Both these scholars deciphered the letter as alpha; but, while the left hasta extends beyond the cross-bar at the bottom, such is also the case with this line in other deltas, notably those of προέδρων in line six, δήμωι in line eight, and ἐπιδοῦναι in line nineteen. If we did not have the context we should certainly read the delta of προέδρων as an alpha. This however, is not the end of the matter. Mr. Dow notes further: "Most of the letter-incisions in this area are plainly marked by discoloration and by the presence of a deposit of brownish matter filling or partially filling the stroke. In fact all the strokes for many centimeters in every direction reveal this deposit to the naked eye except this bar in the controversial letter. This consideration, combined with the fact that the bar makes neither an alpha nor a delta completely sure, suggests that the letter is a lambda, and that the bar is the result of splintering when the stone broke." But we have to proceed yet farther. As an examination of the stone with the aid of a strong magnifying glass discloses, the cross-bar shows faint traces of discoloration (no deposit), and other light strokes (like the cross-bar) lack the brownish deposit. There is none, for example, in a portion of the omikron of προέδρων in line six. Moreover, as can be seen from other fractures of the surface, the stone, when broken, flakes and does not splinter: the grain is very fine and tight. Flaking, on the other hand, eliminates the discoloration. Flaking has, it appears, removed a portion of the surface on which this disputed letter was cut: operating obliquely, it has left unimpaired only the upper part of the right hasta and the entire left hasta, leaving only perceptible traces of the lower part of the right hasta and the cross-bar.

Such being the nature of the epigraphical evidence, the restoration D[aidalides] (Kekropis, IX), suggested by De Sanctis (*Riv. di Fil.*, 1923, p. 172) and approved by Roussel (*REA*, 1924, pp. 98 ff.) contains the required ten letters, and is not to be excluded. There is certainly a cross-bar on the stone at present. On the other hand, the prosopographical arguments marshalled by Dinsmoor (pp. 97 f.) to connect Phoryskides, secretary in IG^2 II 791, with the deme Leukonoe are not to be discarded lightly. But so many new Attic names have turned up since Kirchner published his *Prosopographia Attica*, names new for the community as a whole and for specific demes, that the appearance of a Phoryskides in Daidalidai need cause no surprise. The only conclusions I can reach at present are: (1) if the Diomedon of IG^2 II 791 is the Diomedon of *SEG*, II, 9, the *demotikon* of Phoryskides is probably Daidalidai and the *phyle* Kekropis (IX), since the secretaryship was held in the two preceding years by Oineis (VIII) and Akamantis (VII); (2) if the *demotikon* of Phoryskides is Leukonoe, despite the cross-bar, we should assume that the two Diomedons are different. Diomedon, though rare in the *Prosopographia*,[1] is a good Attic name, and a homonymous son of Diomedon I (*SEG*, II, 9) may have held the archonship at a later date.

---

[1] Two new Diomedons have cropped up since the publication of the prosopographical works of Kirchner and Sundwall, viz., Diomedon Dioklein IG^2 II 1954 (306/5 B.C.) and Diomedon in IG^2 II 1582, l. 13 (*paullo post a.* 348/7 B.C.).

My cycle has a place for Diomedon I in 253/2 B.C. and another for Diomedon II in 232/1; (3) if the letter is alpha, Diomedon II may still fall in 232/1 B.C. We are not obliged to conclude that a break in the secretary-cycle occurred after the second archonship in the closed sequence, Polyeuktos, Hieron, Diomedon.

II. ALTERNATE PRIESTLY CYCLES OF ASKLEPIOS

IT is not, I think, too much to say that Dinsmoor's system of secretary-cycles hinges on his scheme of Tribal Cycles of the priests of Asklepios; and it is the corroboration of the one by the other which gives the whole a special appearance of solidity. The primary pivotal point in his priestly cycles is 286/5 B.C., with a priest, Phyleus of Eleusis, from the *phyle* Hippothontis. No one can doubt any longer that this priest belongs in this year. The discovery and publication by Dinsmoor of the new half of IG^2 II 649 have shown both that my earlier date, 288/7 B.C., was wrong and why it was wrong. Beginning with Hippothontis in 286/5 Dinsmoor constructs cycles in unbroken sequence and regularity thence back to 307/6 and forward to 229/8 B.C. In the latter year a break of seven *phylae* occurred,[1] from Akamantis (VII) in 229/8 to Erechtheis (III) in 228/7 B.C.

The break in 228 B.C. is inferred by working back from his second pivotal point, which is really the priest-

---

[1] The seven *phylae* were discriminated against in that they lost their turn to furnish the priest. Had a new priestly cycle been introduced when Ptolemais was created, for which, as we shall see later (*below*, pp. 95 f., 144), there was no ground and is no evidence, it should have begun with Antigonis (I), or Aiantis (XII).

TABLE II

Year	Type	Archon	Secretary	No. of Phyle	No. of Phyle	Priest of Asklepios
					Aigeis	
307/6	OI*	Anaxikrates	Λυσίας Νοθίππου Διομεύς	II		
306/5	O*	Koroibos	Πάμφιλος Διογείτονος Ῥαμνούσιος	XI	5	
305/4	(O)	Euxenippos		12	6	
304/3	O*	Pherekles	Ἐπιχαρῖνος Δημοχάρους Γαργήττιος	I	7	
303/2	I*	Leostratos	Διόφαντος Διονυσοδώρου Φηγούσιος	III	8	
302/1	O*	Nikokles	Νίκων Θεοδώρου Πλωθεύς	IV	9	
301/0	I*	Klearchos	Μνήσαρχ[ος Τιμοστράτ]ου Προβαλίσιος	V	10	
300/9	O	Hegemachos		6	11	
299/8	O*	Euktemon	Θεόφιλος Ξενοφῶντος Κεφαλῆθεν	VII	12	
298/7	I	Mnesidemos		8	1	
297/6	O	Antiphates		9	2	
296/5	O	Nikias	Ἀ[ν]τικράτης Κρατίν[ου Ἀξην]ι[εύς]	X	3	Demagenes
295/4	I	Nikostratos	Δωρόθεος Ἀρ[ιστομάχ]ου Φαληρεύς	XI	4	
294/3	O	Olympiodoros			5	
293/2	O*	Olympiodoros	Λ . . . ων Μιλτιάδου Ἀλωπεκῆθεν	XII	6	
292/1	I*	Philippos	—ς Αἰθαλίδη[ς]	I	7	
291/0	O*	Aristonymos	. . . . .υς Θορα[ιεύς]	II	8	
290/9	O	Charinos		3	9	
289/8	I	Kimon?			10	
288/7	O*	Diokles	Ξενοφῶ[ν Ν]ικέου Ἁλαιεύς	IV		
287/6	O*	Diotimos	Λυσίστρατος [Ἀ]ριστο[μ]άχου Παιανεύς	V		
286/5	I	Isaios		6	X	Phyleus Eleusis

285/4	0*	Euthios	Ναυσιμένης Ναυσικύδου Χολαργεύς	VII			
284/3	1			8			
283/2	0*	Ourios	Εὔξενος Καλλίου Αἰξωνεύς	IX			
282/1	0	. . . .	. . . . ρίωνος Ἐλευσίν[ιος]	X			
281/0	1		-ίδη[ς] Ν[ικων]ος [Ο]ἰ[τραῖος]	XI			
280/9	0	Gorgias?[1]		12			
279/8	0*	Anaxikrates		1			
278/7	1	Demokles		2			
277/6	0	Euboulos		3	II	Onetor	Melite
276/5	0	P[olystratos?]	Κλεαγ[ένης — Ἁλαιεύς]	IV	XI	Xenokritos	Aphidna
275/4	1*	Glaukippos	Εὔθων[ος . . . . κ]ρίτου Μυρρινοῦσιος	V	XII	-sides	Alopeke
274/3	0*	Xenophon?		VI	1	Nikomachos?	
273/2	1	Telokles?	. . . . ου Σουνιε[ύς]	7	II	Lysanias	Melite
272/1	0			8	III	Smikythos	Anagyrus
271/0	1	Pytharatos		9	4	Ameinias?	
270/9	0*	Peithidemos?		10	V	Lykomedes	Konthyle
269/8	1	Menekles	Θεόδωρος Λυσιθέου Τ[ρ]ι[κ]ο[ρ]ύσιος	XI	VI	—	Sunion
268/7	0*	Nikias Otr.	Ἰσοκράτης Ἰσοκράτου Ἁλωπεκῆθεν	XII	VII	Timokles	Eiresidai
267/6	0			1	VIII	Archikles	Lakiadai
266/5	1*	Philokrates	Ἡγήιππος Ἀριστομάχου Μελιτεύς	II	IX	Lysikles	Sypalettos
265/4	0	[Philipp]ides??		3	X	Prokles	Piraeus
264/3	(O)	Diognetos		4	XI	Lykeas	Rhamnus
263/2	(I)	Antipatros		5	XII	Phileas	Eitea

[23]

TABLE II (*Continued*)

Year	Type	Archon	Secretary	No. of Phyle	No. of Phyle	Priest of Asklepios
			SCHEME A			
263/2	(I)	Antipatros		11	XII	Kalliades Aigilia
262/1	O*	Arrheneides		12	I	Theoxenos Pergase
261/0	(O)	Sosistratos?	.... ανοπον[πο]ν Π[ο]τά[μιος]	I	II	Theodoros Melite
260/9	(I)	Philostratos		2	III	— Euonymon
259/8	(O)	Phanostratos		3	IV	Philippos Ionidai
258/7	O*	Pheidostratos	...... Κηφι[σοδ]ώρου Ἰκ[αριεύς]	IV	V	Autokles Oa
257/6	OI*	Antimachos	Χαιρ[ι]γένης [Χαι]ριγένου Μυρρινούσιος	V	VI	Philokrates Hekale
256/5	O*	Kleomachos	Ἀ[φ]θόνητος Ἀρχίνου Κήττιος	VI	VII	Praxiteles Eiresidai
255/4	O*	Polyeuktos	Χαιρεφῶν Ἀρχεστράτου Κεφαλῆθεν	VII	8	Ktesonides
254/3	I*	Hieron	Φανύλος Πανφίλου Ὑψίθεν	VIII	IX	Boiskos Phlya
253/2	O*	Diomedon	φορυκίδης Ἀριστομένου Δ[αιδαλίδης]	IX	10	
252/1	(O)	Diogeiton	Θεόδοτος Θεοφίλου Κειριάδης	X	11	
251/0	(I)	Theophemos	Προκλῆς Ἀπ- —	11	12	
250/9	O*	Kydenor [2]	...... ος Λύκου Ἁλωπεκῆθε[ν]	XII	1	
249/8	(O)	Eurykleides	——νους Εἰτ[εαῖος]	I	II	Xypete
248/7	(I)	Lysiades	Ἀριστόμαχος Ἀριστο- —	2	3	
247/6	O*	Olbios?	Κυδίας Τιμωνίδου Εὐωνυμεύς	III	4	
246/5	I*	Kallimedes	[Καλ]λίας Καλλιάδου Πλωθεύς	IV	5	
245/4	O	Lysitheides?		5	6	
244/3	O*	Thersilochos	[Δ]ιόδοτος Διογνήτου Φρεάρριος	VI	7	
243/2	I*	Thymochares?	Σώστρατο[ς] Ἀ[ρι]στ..........	7	8	
242/1	O	Alkibiades??		8	9	

[24]

241/0	I	Philomeos?[3]		9	X	10
240/9	O*	Athenodoros	"Αρκετος 'Αρχίου 'Αμαξαντεύς		XI	11	Kalliades Aigilia
239/8	I*	Charikles	— Εὐανέτου Ραμνούσιος		12	12	Theoxenos Pergase
238/7	O	Lysias			1	1	Theodoros Melite
237/6	O	Kimon			2	2	— Euonymon
236/5	I*	Ekphantos	. . . . ος Δημητρίο[υ] Ἱππoτ[ο]μ[ά]δης		II	3	Philippos Ionidai
235/4	O*	Lysanias	Εὔμηλος Ἐμπεδίωνος Εὐωνυμεύς		III	4	Autokles Oa
234/3	(O)				4	5	Philokrates Hekale
233/2	(I)	Jason?			5	6	Praxiteles Eiresidai
232/1	O	[Diomedon[4]	Φορυκίδης 'Αριστομένου Λ[ευκονοεύς]?		VI]	7	Ktesonides
231/0	(O)				7	8	Boiskos Phlya

Scheme B[5]

263/2	(I)	Antipatros			11	XII	Kalliades Aigilia
262/1	O*	Arrheneides			12	I	Theoxenos Pergase
261/0	(O)	Sosistratos?	. . . . ανοπόν[πο]ν Ποτάμιος		1	II	Theodoros Melite
260/9	(I)	Philostratos			2	III	— Euonymon
259/8	(O)	Phanostratos			3	IV	Philippos Ionidai
258/7	O*	Pheidostratos	. . . . Κηρι[σο]δόρου Ἰκ[αριεύς]		IV	A	Autokles Oa
257/6	OI*	Antimachos	Χαυρ[ι]γένης [Χαι]ργένου Μυρρινούσιος		V	VI	Philokrates Hekale
256/5	O*	Kleomachos	'Α[φ]θόνητος 'Αρχίου Κήττιος		VI	VII	Praxiteles Eiresidai
255/4	(I)				7	8	Ktesonides
254/3	(O)				8	IX	Boiskos Phlya
253/2	(I)				9	10
252/1	(O)	Diogeiton	Θεόδοτος Θεοφίλου Κειριάδης		X	11

[25]

TABLE II (*Continued*)

Year	Type	Archon	Secretary	No. of Phyle	No. of Phyle	Priest of Asklepios
251/0	(O)			11	12	
250/9	(I)			12	1	
249/8	(O)	Lysiades	— -νους Εἰτ[εαῖος]	I	II	—
248/7	(I)	Olbios?	Ἀριστόμαχος Ἀριστο— —	2	3	Xypete
247/6	O*	Kallimedes	Κυδίας Τιμωνίδου Εὐωνυμεύς	III	4	
246/5	I*	Lysitheides?	[Καλ]λίας Καλλιάδου Πλωθεύς	IV	5	
245/4	(O)	Thersilochos	[Δ]ιόδοτος Διογνήτου Φρεάρριος	5	6	
244/3	O*	Polyeuktos	Χαιρεφῶν Ἀρχεστράτου Κεφαλῆθεν	VI	7	
243/2	O*	Hieron	Φαυῖλος Παμφίλου Οἴηθεν	VII	8	
242/1	I*	Diomedon	Φορυσκίδης Ἀριστομένου Δ[αιδαλίδης]	VIII	9	
241/0	O*	Athenodoros	Ἄρκετος Ἀρχίου Ἀμαξαντεύς	IX	10	
240/9	O*	Charikles	— Εὐαινέτου Ῥαμνούσιος	X	11	
239/8	I*	Lysias		XI	12	
238/7	O	Kimon		12	1	
237/6	O	Ekphantos	...... ος Δημητρίο[υ] Ἱπποτ[ο]μ[α]δης	1	2	
236/5	I*	Lysanias	Εὔμηλος Ἐμπεδίωνος Εὐωνυμεύς	II	3	
235/4	O*	Theophemos	Προκλῆς Ἀπ— —	III	4	
234/3	(O)	Kydenor		4	5	
233/2	(I)	Eurykleides		5	6	
232/1	(O)	Jason		6	7	
231/0	(O)			7	8	

A. Undated archons between 256/5 and 244/3 B.C. (six places): Alkibiades, Hagnias?, Lykeas?, Philoneos, Thymochares.

Year		Archon				
230/9	(I)	Heliodoros		8	IX	9
229/8	O*		Χαρίας Καλλίου Ἀθμονεύς			10
228/7	I	Leochares		10	XI	11
227/6	O	Theophilos	Φίλιππος Κηφισοδώρου Ἀφ[ιδναῖος]	XI	XII	12
226/5	I*	Ergochares	Ζωίλος Διφίλο[υ] Ἀλωπεκῆ[θεν]	XII	1	1
225/4	O	Niketes		1	2	2
224/3	O	Antiphilos		2	3	3
223/2	I	Kalli-Menekrates		3	4	4
222/1	O	Thrasyphon	.... τοῦ Παιανεύς	4	V	5
221/0	O*	[Ka]lla[ischros]		V	6	6
220/9	I	Chairephon	Φ............ Κυ]δαντίδης	6	VII	7
219/8	O*	....	Ἀριστοτέλης Θεαινέτου Κε[φαλῆθεν]	VII	VIII	8
218/7	O*	Euandros	[Θ]έρσ[ιππος Θ]ρασι[ππον Ἀχαρνεύς]	VIII	IX	9
217/6	I	Pantias?[6]		IX	10	X Timokles Halai
216/5	O	Diokles	Ἀριστοφάνης Στρατοκλέους Κειριάδης	10	XI	11
215/4	I*	Euphiletos		XI	12	XII Eustratos Oinoe
214/3	O	Herakleitos		12	13	13
213/2	O	Archelaos[7]	Μόσχος Μο[σχίωνος Ἀ]νκυλῆθεν	13	I	1
212/1	I*	Aischron		I	2	2
211/0	O			2	3	3
210/9	O			3	4	4
209/8	I*		Ἀρχικλ[ῆς Χ]αριδήμου Ἐρχιεύς[8]	IV	5	5
208/7	O			5	6	6
207/6	(O)			6	7	7
206/5	(I)	Kallistratos	Ἀγνωνίδης Ἀπατουρ[ίο]υ —	7	8	8
205/4	O			8	9	9

[27]

TABLE II (*Continued*)

Year	Type	Archon	Secretary	No. of *Phyle*	No. of *Phyle*	Priest of Asklepios
204/3			..... Ἱερ .. ένωνος Ἐπικηφίσιος	IX	10	
203/2				10	11	
202/1				11	12	
201/0		—		12	13	
201/0				5	1	
200/9				6	2	
199/8				7	3	
198/7				8	4	
197/6				9	5	
196/5				10	6	
195/4				11	7	
194/3				12	8	
193/2		....	.... s Μενεστράτου Λαμπτρεύς	I	9	
192/1				2	10	
191/0				3	11	
190/9				4	12	
189/8	O*	-tes?	— -οδήμου [Αἰ]γιλιεύς	V	1	
188/7	I*	Symmachos	Ἀρχικλῆς Θεοδώρου Θορίκιος	VI	2	
187/6	O	Theoxenos		7	3	
186/5	I*	Zopyros	Μεγάριστος Πύρρου Αἰξωνε[ύ]ς	VIII	4	
185/4	O*	Eupolemos	Στράτωνικος Στρατονίκ[ου Ἀμα]ξαντεύς	IX	5	
184/3	(I)			10	6	

183/2	(O)	Hermogenes		11		7
182/1	O	Timesianax	— 'Αρι]στομάχου Προβαλίσιος	XII		8
181/0	I*		— ἐκ Κ]ηδῶν?	I		9
180/9	O			2		10
179/8	O			3		11
178/7	I	Philon		4		12
177/6	O			5		1
176/5	O	Hippakos		6		2
175/4	I*	Sonikos	Παυσανίας Βιό[ττ]ον Περιθοίδης	VII		3
174/3	O			8		4
173/2	(O)			9		5
172/1	(I)	Sosigenes		10		6
171/0	O*	Antigenes	Σώσανδρος — 'Αλωπεκῆθεν	XI		7
170/9	I			12		8
169/8	O*	Eunikos	Ἱερώνυμος Βοήθον Κηφισιεύς	I		9
168/7	I	Xenokles	Σθενέδημος Ἀσκληπιάδον Τειθράσιος	II		10
167/6	O	Nikosthenes?		3		11
166/5	I*	Achaios	Ἡρακλέων Ναννάκου Εὐπυρίδης	IV		12
165/4	O*	Pelops	Διονυσικλῆς Διονυσίου Ἐκαλῆθεν	V		1
164/3		Epainetos??		6		2
163/2		Erastos		7		3
162/1		Poseidonios		8		4
161/0	O*	Aristolas	. . . . . . s Φιλωνίδου Ἐλευσίνιος	IX		5
160/9	I*	Tychandros	Σωσιγ[έ]νης Μενεκράτου Μαρ[αθώνιος]	X	Protagoras Pergase	6
159/8	O			11		7
158/7				12		8

[29]

TABLE II (*Continued*)

Year	Type	Archon	Secretary	No. of Phyle	No. of Phyle	Priest of Asklepios
157/6		Anthesterios				
156/5		Kallistratos				
155/4		Mnesitheos				
154/3		Aristaichmos?				
153/2		Phaidrias?				
152/1						
151/0						
150/9						
149/8						
148/7		Lysiades?				
147/6	O*	Archon				
146/5	OI	Epikrates	— — Συπαλήττιος	VIII		
145/4	O*	Metrophanes	Ἐπιγένης Μοσχίωνος Λαμπτρεύς	I	10	
144/3	O*	E- (Hermias?)[9]		2	11	
143/2	I	Theaitetos	Φιλ- — — [Παα]νιεύς?	3	12	
142/1	O	Aristophon		4	1	
141/0	O	Dionysios?	— — [B]ουτάδης	V	2	
140/9	I	Hagnotheos	Μενεκράτης Χαριξένου Θορίκιος	VI	3	
139/8	O*	Apollodoros	. . . . .νος Ὀηθεν	VII	4	
138/7	O	Timarchos		8	V	
137/6	I*	Herakleitos	Διονύσ[ιο]ς Δημητρίου Ἀνακαιεύς	IX	6	Zoilos Phlya
136/5	O	Timarchides		10	7	
135/4	(O)	Ergokles?		11	8	

[30]

134/3	(I)	Epikles?	[Γοργ]ίλος Γοργίλου Ἀ-	12	9	
133/2	O	Xenon		1	10	
132/1	I*	Mikion?	Κέφαλος Κεφάλου [Κυδαντίδης]?	II	11	
131/0	O	Nikomachos?		3	12	
130/9	I	Demostratos		4	1	
129/8	O	Lykiskos		5	2	
128/7	I*	Dionysios	Ἰάσων Ἀριστοκ[ράτου Χολαργεύς]?	VI	3	
127/6	O	Theodorides		7	4	
126/5		Diotimos	Συ— — —	8	5	
125/4		Jason	Ἀθην[όδωρος?] Ἀναξικράτους Ἐλευσίνιος	IX	6	
124/3		Nikias and Isigenes				
123/2		Demetrios		10	7	
122/1	O*	Nikodemos	Ἐπιγένης Ἐπιγένου Οἰναῖος	11	8	
121/0	I	Phokion?	Εὔανδρος — —	XII	9	
120/9	O	Eumachos	— -[δ]ότου Διομεευ[s]?	1	10	
119/8	I	Hipparchos		II	11	
118/7	O*	Lenaios	Ἰσίδωρος Ἀπολλωνίου Σκαμβωνίδης	3	12	
117/6	O	Menoites		IV	1	
116/5	I*	Sarapion	Σοφο[κλ]ῆς Δημητ[ρίο]υ Ἰφιστιάδης	5	2	
115/4	O	Nausias		VI	3	
114/3		Pleistainos?		7	4	Leonides Phlya?
113/2		Paramonos		8	V	
112/1	O*	Dionysios	Λάμιος Τιμοίχου Ραμνούσιος	9	6	
111/0		Sosikrates	— -ρος Κρωιεύς	X	7	
110/9		Polykleitos		XI	8	
109/8	O*	Jason	Ἐπιφάνης Ἐπιφάνου Λαμπτρεύς	12	9	
				1	I	Nikodoros Kephisia

[31]

TABLE II (Continued)

Year	Type	Archon	Secretary	No. of Phyle	No. of Phyle	Priest of Asklepios
108/7	I	Demochares	— Διονυσοδώρου Ἀγκυλ[ῆθεν]	II	2	
107/6	O*	Aristarchos	Τελέστης Μηδείου Παιανιεύς	III	3	
106/5	O*	Agathokles	Εὔκλης Ξενάνδρου Αἰθα[λίδη]ς	IV	4	
105/4	I	Herakleides?		5	5	
104/3	O	Theodotos?		6	VI	Philemon Hermos?
103/2	O*	Theokles	-θέτης Κλεινίου Κοθωκί[δης]	VII	7	
102/1	I	Echekrates		8	8	
101/0	O*	Medeios	Φιλίων Φιλίωνος Ἐλευσίνιος	IX	9	
100/9		Theodosios		10	10	
99/8		Prokles		11	11	
98/7		Argeios		12	12	
97/6		Argeios				
96/5		Herakleitos	-της Ἐπ- —	1	1	
95/4		Diokles?		2	2	
94/3		Isokrates?		3	3	
93/2		Kallias		4	4	
92/1		Menedemos?	— — —τιος? (IG² II 1054)	5	5	
91/0		Medeios				
90/9		Medeios				
89/8		Medeios				
88/7		Anarchia				
87/6		Philanthes			1	
86/5		Hierophantes			2	

[32]

85/4	Pythokritos?	3	
84/3	Aischraios?	4	
83/2	Seleukos?	V	Embrios Prospalta?
82/1	Herakleodoros?	6	
81/0	Apollodoros?	7	
80/9		8	
79/8		9	
78/7		10	
77/6		11	
76/5		12	
75/4	Aischines?	I	Menandros Kephisia?
74/3		2	
73/2		3	
72/1		IV	Ameipsias Potamos?
71/0		5	
70/9		6	
69/8		7	
68/7		8	
67/6		9	
66/5		X	Apollodoros Rhamnus?
65/4		11	
64/3		12	
63/2	. . . ios	I	Sokrates Kephisia
62/1	Aristaios	II	Theodoros Myrrhinoutta
61/0	Theophemos	3	
60/9	Herodes	4	
59/8	Leukios	5	

[33]

TABLE II (*Concluded*)

Year	Type	Archon	Secretary	No. of Phyle	No. of Phyle	Priest of Asklepios
58/7		Kalliphon			6	
57/6		Diokles			7	
56/5		Kointos			8	
55/4		Aristodemos			9	
54/3		Zenon			10	
53/2		Diodoros			11	
52/1		Lysandros	Γάϊος Γαΐου Ἁλαιεύς	II or VIII	12	Diokles Kephisia
51/0		Lysiades			I	
50/9		Demetrios			2	
49/8		Demochares	— -στοκλέους Ἀπολλωνιεύς	XII	3	
48/7		Philokrates			4	

A. Undated archons: before 271/0 b.c., [Ape]llaios; in 234/3–230/29, Hagnias (secretary, Ποτάμων Δοr-), Lykeas; before or after 200, . . . bios, Dionysios, Dionysios (secretary, Θεολύτος —-[θ]εν), -es, Nikophon, Phanarchides (secretary for following archonship, Προκλῆς Περι-), Philinos, Proxenides (secretary, Εὐβούλος Εὐβουλί[δου]). . . . . s (secretary, [Θε]οδόσιος Ξενοφα[ν]-), -s (secretary, Νικ[άν]ορ); in 174/3–170/69, Alexandros; in 159/8–147/6, Andreas, Aristophantos, Diokles, Zaleukos; in 80/79–64/3, Aristoxenos, Kriton, Medeios, Niketes, -os, Theoxenos, Zenion; in the general period, Andronides, Aristeides.

B. Other secretaries: in the third century, — [Ἀρισ]τ[οδ]ή[μ]ο[υ] or [Ἀρισ]τ[ομ]ή[δ]ο[υ] (*IG* II² 738, cf. add.), [Κηφ]ισοκλ[ῆς] (*IG*² II 800), -ν Ἀγροθέου (*IG*² II 815), Σημ[ω]νίδη[ς] (*IG*² II 816), ——-ς (*IG*² II 861); in 157/6–147/6, —— [Ἐ]ρμεος (*IG*² II 989); in ca. 100, Δημήτριος Δημ- (*IG*² II 1027).

C. An asterisk indicates that the calendar quality of a year is determined definitely; brackets that an alternate arrangement of ordinary and intercalary years is possible.

NOTES TO TABLE II

[1] Gorgias belongs either in 281/0 or 280/79 B.C. His name has been restored by Dinsmoor (pp. 72 f.) in IG^2 II 773; but this involves a line of 24 letters, whereas one of at least 25 is required. It also brings the second gamma where this letter is impossible. Mr. Dow reads ['Eπὶ] . . ρ.ι.ο[υ]. The rho (formerly read as omikron) is "almost certain": the circle seems too small and too high in the line to be an omikron. As he will show in an article to be published shortly, IG^2 II 773 belongs to the year of Koroibos (306/5 B.C.), where it fits perfectly. This removal of IG^2 II 773 from the archonship of Gorgias permits us to assign IG^2 II 670B to the year immediately following that of IG^2 II 670A, as is desirable.

[2] With Wilhelm's suggested restoration, [Kydenor]ος, in *SEG*, III, 122 (*Attische Urkunden*, III: *Sitz. Wien. Akad.*, CCII 5, 1925, p. 15; cf. *Hermes*, 1927, pp. 489 f.; Dinsmoor, p. 178) we cannot place Kydenor in 233/2 B.C. (Table II, Scheme B); for at the time Antigonus was king of Macedon.

[3] On Dinsmoor's premises (p. 85), restoring Αἰξωνεύς instead of Αἰθαλίδης in IG^2 II 794, Hagnias (IG^2 II 1292) may belong in 241/0 B.C. His name could then be restored in IG^2 II 1290. But Lykeas (IG^2 II 1284) can also be restored in IG^2 II 1290, in which case he belonged either in this year or in 230/29 B.C., these being the only intercalary years available (Lykeas, however, may belong before 263/2 B.C.). Dinsmoor dates Hagnias in 267/6 B.C. and Olbios in 276/5. He has no room for them in the middle of the third century, where the letter-forms seem to place them. The secretary for Olbios' year came from Euonymon (new inscription from the agora). The years open for Olbios are, accordingly, 266/5 and 247/6 B.C. The prosopographical evidence is all we have to go by, and it does not enable us to choose definitely between them. Amynomachos of Bate, mover in his year of a decree of the Mesogeia in honor of Polyeuktos of Bate (IG^2 II 1245), was one of the heirs of Epicurus, who died in 271/0 B.C. He was presumably a much younger man than the philosopher. The daughter of Polyeuktos, a married woman, dedicated some objects to Athena Polias, of whom she was priestess, in the archonship of Alkibiades (IG^2 II 776). Alkibiades was archon during the Macedonian epoch, 263/2–230/29 B.C. (Dinsmoor, p. 171). In Alkibiades' year an inventory of the votive offerings on the Acropolis was drawn up (*Pollux*, X, 126). There is a slight presumption, based on fourth-century practice (*Treasurers of Athena*, pp. 14; 111, n. 4; 117, n. 1; 119, n. 1; 123; 124 and n. 2), that his was a Great Panathenaic year. The possible years for him are 247/6, 242/1 or 241/0, and, leaving one year for Jason, 234/3–230/29 B.C. It is less likely that Polyeuktos of Bate was active politically in 266/5 B.C., at the time of the Chremonidean War, than in 247/6 B.C., seeing that he was a man of prominence during the Macedonian epoch. I

have, accordingly, assigned Olbios tentatively to 247/6 B.C., and I suggest 242/1 or 234/3 for Alkibiades. 230/29, the other Great Panathenaic year, seems excluded by the references to the Macedonian royal family in IG^2 II 776, since this decree was probably passed near the end of the year, and by the end of 230/29 B.C. Athens had already revolted from Demetrius.

[4] I have entered Phoryskides twice, here and in 253/2 B.C. For the reason see *above*, pp. 18 f.; *below*, p. 88.

[5] For the reasons for inserting in Table II an alternative scheme of archons for the period 263/2–230/29 B.C., see below, pp. 114 ff.

[6] The space in IG^2 II 1706, col. ii, l. 89 is too short for Pantiades (Patiades, Pasiades), according to Kirchner (IG^2 II 849, note), whom my reading of the squeeze confirms; hence Wilamowitz (*Hermes*, 1928, pp. 377 f.; cf. Kirchner, IG^2 II 1706, note) suggested Pantias on the analogy of the archon for 480/79 B.C., who is sometimes called Kallias and at other times Kalliades (*PA*, 7773). For the various readings of the text of Philodemos (*Ind. Acad. Herc.*, col. 27, Jacoby, *FGH*, II B, 244, 47), which alone gives us the name, see Dinsmoor, p. 48, n. 7. It is also possible, but less likely, that Pantiades belongs, not ten years before Kallistratos (206/5 B.C.), but immediately before or after him (Beloch, *Griech. Gesch.*, IV, 2, p. 558; cf. Jacoby, *FGH*, II BD, p. 740).

[7] Since Ankyle was transferred only in part from Aigeis to Antigonis, Archelaos may belong in 209/8 B.C. I have preferred the earlier date, seeing that, when everything is said (*Hell. Ath.*, p. 256, n. 3; Dinsmoor, p. 219, n. 3), Pausanias' collocation (II, 9, 4) of the death of Eurykleides and Mikion with that of Aratos, who died in 213 B.C., is more easily intelligible if the demise of the Athenian statesmen occurred in *ca.* 211 B.C. rather than eight years later.

[8] The decree from which this secretary comes was found at Magnesia (Kern, *Inschr. von Magnesia*, no. 37). Kirchner (IG^2 II iv, p. 14) dates it in 222/1 B.C.; but, from its content — the reception by Athens of the Leukophryena — it cannot precede 221/0 B.C., the year in which the Magnesians received the oracle requiring them to establish this fête. Since the formula of dating shows that it belonged to the epoch of the 13 *phylae* (Dinsmoor, p. 209), and since the names of the Magnesian *theori* mentioned in it demonstrate that it must antedate the loss of Chalcis by Philip in 199 B.C. (*Inschr. von Magnesia*, no. 47; cf. *below*, p. 128, n. 1), the only alternative is 209/8 B.C. 209/8 B.C. suits the conditions admirably. See further, *below*, pp. 95, 128 ff., and notes.

[9] In suggesting Hermias in IG^2 II 2323, col. vi, l. 252 Dinsmoor (p. 468) leans heavily on the computation of the space occupied by the archon-name as six letters. Kirchner now computes it at nine. If the predecessor of this archon was Aristophon (Kirchner), we may restore Dionysios (Dinsmoor, pp. 268 f.).

tamias, weighing 130+ drachmas; a *hedypotion* attributed to the priest Smikythos of Anagyrus, of which the description is broken away; another *hedypotion* attributed to the priest Xenokritos of Aphidna, made from the *typi*, weighing 29 drachmas; another *hedypotion* attributed to the priest Lykomedes of Konthyle, made from the *typi*, weighing 34 drachmas; an object attributed to a priest from Sunion, made from the *typi*, weighing 19 drachmas, 3 obols; and a *skaphion* attributed to the priest Archikles of Lakiadai, made from the *typi*, weighing 33 drachmas. The uniqueness of this entry is obvious on the most cursory reading of the inventory. Otherwise vessels made from *typi* were dedicated by the priests during their term of office or in the year immediately following: by Lysikles (266/5) in the year of Prokles, 265/4; by Theodoros (261/0) in his own year; by Autokles (258/7) in the year of Philokrates, 257/6; by Philokrates (257/6) in his own year; by Praxiteles (256/5), if at all, in a year covered by a *lacuna;* by Ktesonides (255/4) in his own year; and by Boiskos? (254/3) in his own year. Obviously, it was customary for the priests to have a lot of little silver *typi* melted down either near or at the end of their year and to hand over the vessel made from the metal thus secured as soon as it was finished. At the end of 264/3 B.C., on the other hand, such vessels made by ex-priests and theretofore in priestly use were inventoried in a block. It can hardly be an accident that the year at the close of which this occurred was the last of the pre-Antigonid regime. (3) For the first time a *tetrachmon Antigoneion* appears in the inventory in the priesthood of Theoxenos (262/1), the year immediately following the capture of

Athens by Antigonus. Subsequently *tetrachma Antigoneia* appear in Philippos' year (259/8), in Praxiteles' year (256/5), and in Ktesonides' year (255/4). It is to be noted in this connection that one of the issues of these coins was apparently minted in Athens. (4) A dedication to Asklepios made by the *demos*, Antibios being *tamias*, appears in Lykeas' year (264/3) and not again till Philokrates' (257/6). It appears yearly thereafter — in 254/3 it can have been lost. The gap between 264/3 and 257/6 B.C. is probably significant. It is not likely that the four *hedypotia* entered in 264/3 at the end of Lykeas' list were received by the temple in that year: they then appear among "the silver vessels which the priests were using." That is to say, they were doubtless a presentation of an earlier time; and since the *demos* seems not to have made a gift to the Asklepieion in 266/5 or 265/4 B.C., we can assume, what is in itself probable, that it had other uses for its money during the Chremonidean War. Antibios was obviously *tamias* in 264/3, the year in which the four *hedypotia*, each a gift of a separate year doubtless, were entered among the dedications as being withdrawn from priestly use. Two other gifts of the *demos* are recorded in frg. π, which, judging from the spacing of the letters, belongs near the top of the stone; they were probably in priestly use at the time the inventory was made. Assigning one of these six gifts of the *demos* to each year preceding the beginning of the Chremonidean War in 270/69 B.C. (Dinsmoor), we reach 276/5 B.C. as the year of the first presentation. As we shall see later, that is a significant conclusion. It detracts somewhat from the neatness of this observation that the *demos* resumed the practice of making an annual gift to Asklepios in 257/6 B.C.; but we can, I believe, assume that Athens had sufficiently recovered from the post-war depression by the year preceding the withdrawal by Antigonus of the garrison in the Museum to enable it once again to make a public dedication to Asklepios. The *demos* transacted business all the while the "city" was held by Antigonus (*Diog. Laert.*, VII 10; IG^1 II 1199, cf. II^2 iv, p. 15; IG^2 II 477?; IG^2 II 734, cf. Dinsmoor, p. 173; IG^2 II 767?; 768–770; IG^1 II 1349).

As Tarn asseverates (*Antigonos Gonatas*, p. 421), these coincidences "cannot be accidental"; and they are none the less impressive now that they are adjusted to the rectified date for the capture of Athens. Moreover, we can confirm them by a closer study both of the inventory on which they are based and of the inventory which precedes it on the obverse of the stone (IG^2 II 1534A).

III. The Relation of Priestly Tribal Cycles to Inventories

Assuming that the years assigned to the priests Lysikles — Boiskos are correct, the inventory of Boiskos must be that of the last complete year of the entire catalogue, since the decree authorizing the *exetasmos* of the dedications in the Asklepieion was passed in the sixth prytany of the archonship of Diomedon (ll. 141, 162), whom my secretary-cycle, now confirmed by new evidence (*above*, pp. 16 ff; *below*, pp. 52, 75 ff.), places in the year 253/2 B.C. Are there any indications that this was so? It is clear that when the stone fails us the inventory on the obverse was drawing to a close: its main portion (ll. 167–187) as the first part of the chronological catalogue by priests, thus enlarging the number of priests before Lysikles to eight or thereabouts. But to me this seems inadmissible. Manifestly the inventory opened with a list of articles used in worship ([κειμή]λια? πρὸς τὴν χρείαν τῷ [ἱε]ρεῖ καὶ τοῖς [θύουσιν], l. 167, repeated in ll. 152, 182). The objects inventoried in frg. *ab* are cult-articles and their weights are normally correspondingly large: they find their analogues in the rest of the inventory only in the vessels made by priests and ex-priests from the *typi* and the dedications of the *demos*. They correspond in character with the articles listed in 1534A at the end of the main catalogue under the titles "these are the articles of silver in the possession of the priest," "these are the (other) articles in the possession of the priest." We have, accordingly, no right to assume that the yearly catalogue by priests began before line 187. But since we do not know the extent of the gap at this point there may have been eight or more annual inventories before that of Lysikles in 266/5 B.C. We have no basis of computation — as yet. All we can be reasonably sure of is that there were at least four or five.

Assuming that there was no gap at all, the first priest in the chronological list would belong in 271/0 or 270/69; but, if we want to, we can assign all the ex-priests mentioned in the inventory to years and thus make 276/5 B.C. its beginning. And this is undoubtedly the logical thing to do. The inventory began in the archonship of P- (l. 145);[1] and it happens that in

[1] Subsequently the suggestion will be made that the name was Polystratos (pp. 81 ff.).

271/0 B.C. Pytharatos was archon and in 270/69 Peithidemos (Dinsmoor, p. 160). Either would suit, but only if there was no gap at all between frg. *ab* and frg. *c-k*, and only when we should assume that five or six ex-priests held office outside the period covered by the inventory.

Omitting for the moment the ex-priests responsible for the "silver vessels which the priests used" until 263/2 B.C. and the priests of the chronological series, the following priests are mentioned in the inventory: l. 186, —; l. 197, Amein- (τύπος, ἱερεὺς Ἀμειν-); l. 202, Timokles of Eiresidai (τύπος, ἱερεὺς Τιμοκλῆ Εἰ[ρεσίδ]). The priest of line 186 may be responsible for some article used in worship. The others are doubtless predecessors, at no great distance, of Lysikles, and Timokles can, in fact, be assigned to 268/7 B.C.

The problem is what to do with the eight ex-priests of lines 219–222. The *demotika* of seven of them are known. They all belong to different *phylae*. That can hardly be accidental. Arranged in the official order — we are warranted in arranging them thus because of the use of the official order after 266/5 B.C. — they can be placed as in Table II (see p. 23). It follows that IG^2 II 1534B covered precisely two Tribal Cycles, beginning in 276/5 B.C., where, on this assumption, we should place an archon whose name began with P, and ending in 253/2 in the archonship of Diomedon. Let us hold fast to that conclusion. It harmonizes with general practice in Athens thus to observe fixed cycles in timing administrative changes, completing inventories, and recording lists of magistrates. Notoriously the Panathenaic periods were decisive in such matters for the *tamiae* of Athena (*Treasurers of Athena, passim*); and, as is pointed out below (pp. 90 f.), the Tribal Cycles served similarly to set limits to administrative usages and secretarial activities in other services. It happens, moreover, that on the next occasion when we know definitely that the *ex-votos* in the Asklepieion were taken and melted down for the renovation of the cult-apparatus, this too was done at the end (with Hippothontis in 216/5 B.C.) of the priestly cycle of Asklepios (IG^2 II 1539, Diokles archon, 215/4 B.C.).[1]

The next problem is: what is the relation between 1534A and 1534B? Are they directly continuous or does an interval elapse between them? The tablet, of course, stood with its reverse blank from the archonship following that of Eu- (l. 8) to the archonship of Diomedon (253/2 B.C.); and it is, therefore, conceivable that in the meanwhile an inventory or inventories had been posted on the obverse or obverses of other *stelae*, and that it was only in 253/2 B.C. that the commissioners determined to begin using reverses. For such a procedure parallels can readily be found (*Treasurers of Athena*, pp. 69 ff.). But it is much more natural to assume, as is commonly done, that the two inventories (from the front and back of the same *stele*) were consecutive. To be acceptable the contrary would have to be proved. The point would be proved if Phyleus of Eleusis, priest in 286/5 B.C., appeared in 1534A, which

---

[1] The priestly cycles inaugurated in 276/5 B.C. were thus observed for at least five cycles. We can assign IG^2 II 1536 to an inventory made in 240/39 or 228/7 B.C. and IG^2 II 1537 to an inventory made in 202/1 B.C. The chances are that the cycles beginning with Aiantis and ending with Hippothontis were observed in the second century also (cf. *below*, p. 174).

is not the case; or if there were no possibility of his having appeared in 1534A, which is again not the case: his name can be restored in line 43 (Ph-), or it can have appeared in the gap between frg. *ab* and frg. *c–k*, or elsewhere.

IG^2 II 1534A was issued in a year in which Kleigenes was secretary and which was preceded immediately by one in which Eu- was archon. 277/6 B.C. is free for Eu-, completed Eubulos (IG^2 II 682, l. 58; cf. Dinsmoor, pp. 77 ff.), and 276/5 B.C. for Kleigenes, who can then be given his most appropriate *demotikon*, Halaieus (Dinsmoor, p. 160), and be assigned to the *phyle* Aigeis— the right *phyle* for this year. But there are other archons whose names begin with Eu- to be taken into account, viz., Euthios (285/4), Euktemon (299/8), and (omitting Euxenippos, 305/4, who is excluded because of Kleigenes) Euthykritos (328/7) and Euainetos (335/4). The two latter must be rejected. IG^2 II 1534A contains the names of 18+ priests. There are not enough years for so many priests between the terminal year of IG^2 II 1533 (which lists the priests between 341/0 B.C. and 336/5+ B.C.) and 328/7 B.C. Euthios (286/5 B.C.), on the other hand, is too near P- (276/5 B.C.) to admit of a whole inventory intervening between IG II^2 1534A and 1534B. Euktemon (299/8 B.C.) is unobjectionable — unless Kleigenes belongs to Halai.

There is, however, another approach to the problem. As pointed out by me (*Treasurers of Athena*, pp. 124 ff.), the practice existed between 322/1 (or 331/0) and 305/4 B.C. of melting down the silver votives in the Asklepieion yearly and at short intervals and depositing with the *tamiae* of Athena on the Acropolis the ves-

sels made from the proceeds.¹ In the epoch of 18+
years preceding the archonship after that of Eu- this
practice was non-existent: the votives of silver and gold
were then allowed to accumulate in the Asklepieion to
be catalogued at the termination of the period. This
excludes Euktemon and probably Euthios also.

The conclusion seems cogent (admitting the premises) that IG^2 II 1534A preceded 1534B directly. It
then follows that 1534B began early enough to accommodate all the ex-priests mentioned in it who preceded
Lysikles in 266/5 B.C. Otherwise they could hardly
have failed to appear in 1534A. And this conclusion is
corroborated by the observation that in 1534A we
have no reference to the practice prevalent in 1534B
and followed by the earliest ex-priest, Xenokritos of
Aphidna (l. 221), of dedicating vessels made from *typi*.
Yet had this practice existed it could not have failed
to show traces in this inventory. Clearly there was no
overlapping of IG^2 II 1534A and 1534B.² In the nature
of the case the two inventories must be mutually exclusive: objects catalogued in the one could not appear in the other, and priests serving within the limits
of the one could not be responsible for dedications
listed in the other. We must, therefore, suppose that
the practice for the priests to combine the little *typi* so

[1] The great weights of these vessels (1000–1500 drachmas; cf. IG^2 II 1492, ll. 22 ff., *Treasurers of Athena*, p. 125, n. 1) distinguish them from the articles made later by the priests from *typi*.

[2] Dinsmoor has to postulate an overlapping of two years. He can avoid the difficulty that Xenokritos and -sides should have appeared in IG^2 II 1534A by assuming that they may have appeared in the gaps, specifically in the gap at the end of the inventory assumable by his dating of Boiskos four years before the archon Diomedon. The overlapping of the two inventories remains.

TRIBAL CYCLES AND INVENTORIES

as to make single vessels of a more massive and useful character was inaugurated at the time of the *exetasmos* in the second prytany of P-'s archonship in 276/5 B.C.

We have already seen that the first of the ex-priests in IG^2 II 1534B, Xenokritos of Aphidna, belongs in 276/5 B.C. It is now to be noted that prior to his priesthood precisely four priestly cycles, 288/7-277/6, 300/299-289/8, 312/1-301/0, and 322/1-313/2, carry us back to 322/1 B.C. At 322/1 B.C. we join the cycle of priests of Asklepios (and prytany-secretaries) already established for the fourth century (*Priests of Asklepios*, pp. 131 ff.; Dinsmoor, pp. 452 ff.). We may also link the cycles beginning in 276/5 B.C. with those followed in 356/5-322/1 B.C. in a different way. We can assume that in 321/0-308/7 B.C. we have 14 years of allotted or irregular order;[1] that in 307/6 B.C. Aigeis was given the priesthood of Asklepios as well as the prytany-secretariat and possibly the priesthood of Artemis Kalliste (see *below*, p. 64, n. 1), thus continuing the cycle in official order which began with Erechtheis in 322/1 B.C. and was interrupted by the establishment of Antipater's oligarchy in 321 B.C.; that, accordingly, Aiantis held the priesthood in 300/299 B.C.; that rotation by allottment was introduced in 288 B.C. (after Hippothontis had held the office in 289/8 B.C.), at the time of the revolt from Demetrius; and that rotation in the fixed order was resumed, as was right, with Aiantis in 276/5 B.C. On either construction we have cyclic continuity between 356/5 and 276/5 B.C.

[1] We can imagine, for example, that the order was irregular during the oligarchy in 321/0-319/8 B.C.; that a tribal cycle of fixed or allotted order existed in 318/7-309/8 B.C., and that Erechtheis held the priesthood in 308-7 B.C.; but we have no facts to go by.

IV. Tribal Cycles with Allotted Order of *Phylae*

BEFORE proceeding farther it must be observed that the Athenians employed two methods of distributing a function or an office in rotation among the *phylae*. The one best known was that used in assigning the tribal prytanies to the successive fractions of the year (tenths prior to 307/6 B.C., twelfths between 307/6 and 224/3 B.C., thirteenths between 223/2 and 201 B.C., elevenths in 201/0 B.C., and twelfths from 200 B.C. to the time of Hadrian) — sortition. The other was the method of rotation in the official order of the *phylae* or, as prior to 356 B.C., its reverse. The effect of each was the same — the equalization of the *phylae* and hence of all Athenians (for the *phylae* were theoretically, if not actually, cf. *Rev. de Phil.*, 1929, pp. 179 ff., equal in size) in the opportunity of administrative service. Since I first discovered that the latter method was used for the prytany-secretaries, the secretaries of the *tamiae*, and the priests of Sarapis at Delos (*The Athenian Secretaries*), it has been found to have been employed more widely — for the priests of Asklepios (*The Priests of Asklepios*, pp. 131 ff.; Sundwall, *Epigraphische Beitraege zur sozial-politischen Geschichte Athens im Zeitalter des Demosthenes*, pp. 47 f.), the priests of Artemis Kalliste (*Klio*, 1907, p. 213), the priests of the Great Gods at Delos (*Klio*, 1907, pp. 215 ff.; Roussel, *Délos*, pp. 348 ff.), other Delian priests (Dinsmoor, pp. 240 ff.), and the secretaries of the *Hellenotamiae* (Meritt, *ap.* Ferguson, *Treasurers of Athena*, p. 10, n. 1); and it is doubtless capable of yet farther extension (*below*, p. 160,

n. 1). The alternate method was not confined to the allocation of the prytanies to the sections of the year. It has been shown that prior to 356/5 B.C. it was used to determine the tribal sequence between 366/5 and 357/6 B.C. of the prytany-secretaries (*Klio*, 1914, pp. 393 ff.; Dinsmoor, p. 351 and n. 4); it was probably used to distribute the clerkship of the *tamiae* of Athena among the *phylae* during three cycles, 385/4–356/5 B.C. (*Treasurers of Athena*, pp. 142 ff.);[1] and I shall point out later (pp. 145 ff., 162 ff.) that it was doubtless used for the priesthood of Hagne Aphrodite at Delos, and, as an alternate for the official order, for one cycle (157/6–146/5 B.C.) of prytany-secretaries, priests of Asklepios, priests of Sarapis, priests of the Great Gods, and priests of Zeus Kynthios. The practice of the Council in distributing its prytanies by sortition made it familiar at all times to the Athenians and it must be thought of as substitutable at any moment for rotation in the fixed order. I am inclined to think that when, if ever, the evidence becomes sufficiently complete to enable us to ascertain the facts, we shall discover that tribal rotation by one or other of these two methods was used for all the annual offices filled by allotment; and, indeed, in one instance at least, when an office was held by five men (the Delian Amphictyons), tribal rotation was secured by assigning the charge alternately to the first five and the last five *phylae* in the official order (*Class. Rev.*, 1901, pp. 38 ff.). Sortition, conjoined with tribal

---

[1] Cf., however, Dinsmoor, *AJA*, 1932, pp. 163 ff. Dinsmoor maintains that the fixed sequence in reverse order was maintained (with two secretaries in the year 377/6 B.C.) till 358/7 B.C., when the cycles in regular order beginning with Erechtheis were started.

rotation, of administrative offices was fundamental in Athenian government; and oligarchs differed from democrats, not so much as to the principle, as on the practical question of the offices to which it should be applied (*Treasurers of Athena*, pp. 144 ff.).

The evidence substantiates the view that the three senior archonships were also distributed by allotment among the *phylae*. We have really only two lists of these magistrates with which to work, IG^2 II 1706 and 2336; but in the following table the data yielded by isolated lists are appended:

TABLE III

Year	Archon	Phyle[1] of Archon	Phyle of King	Phyle of Polemarch	Phylae of *Thesmothetae*				
IG² II 1706									
230/9									
229/8	Heliodoros	2	8	7	4	5	6 10	11	12
228/7	Leochares	12	5	8	1	4	7 9	10	11
227/6	Theophilos	10	11	8	2	3	5 6	9	12
226/5	Ergochares	7	..	6	1	2	3 9	10	11
225/4	Niketes	6	10	1 or 3	2	4	7 8	9	12
*224/3	Antiphilos	11	2	12	1	3	9 6		
223/2	Kalli-						4 8	10	11
222/1	Menekrates	8	9	12 or 2[2]	1	2	4 6	P	11
221/0	Thrasyphon	12	4	11	1				
220/9	Kallaischros								
219/8	Chairephon								
218/7	....								
217/6	Euandros	..	..	..				11	12
216/5	Pantias?	4	7	6	2	3	5 P	9	11
215/4	Diokles	1	5	10[3]	4	P	7 8	9	12
214/3	Euphiletos	5	10	8	1	3	P 9	11	12
213/2	Herakleitos	9	..	..			7		10

CYCLES WITH ALLOTTED ORDER OF PHYLAE

IG^2 II 2336

103/2	Theokles [4]									
*102/1	Echekrates	..	..	10	9	2	7	4	5	6
101/0	Medeios	9	12	3	1	5	6	7	8	
100/9	Theodosios	7	4	9	1	2	3	5	11	12
99/8	Prokles									
98/7	Argeios	10	6	8	3	5	7	9	11	12
97/6	Argeios									
96/5	Herakleitos	6	2	7	1	3	4	5	10	12

IG^2 II 1714

†ca. 90		..	5	12	2	5	7	8	10	11

IG^2 II 1717

†56/5	Kointos	10	11	9	1	5	6	8	9	11

IG^2 II 1721

14/3	Polyainos	12	4	5	1	2	3	6	8	9

IG^2 II 1722

†ca. 8	Xenon	5	6	7	1	2	3	4	4	7

IG^2 II 1729

†ca. 1		..	..	..	5	6	9	10	10	11

* Years in which the listing of the *thesmothetae* in the official order was disturbed. The irregularity of 102/1 B.C. was obviously due to carelessness. This list was cut on stone partly at the end of 103/2 and partly at the end of 96/5 B.C. (Kirchner, note). The second stone-cutter listed the first three *thesmothetae* of his first year (102/1 B.C.) regardless of their tribal sequence and then switched over to the official order.

† Years in which single *phylae* were represented by two *archontes*.

NOTES TO TABLE III

[1] The number indicates the position of the *phyle* in the official order. In the part of the table which covers the years 223/2–213/2 B.C., however, I have indicated Ptolemais by its initial letter, thus designating the last six *phylae* by the same numbers both before and after 223/2 B.C.

[2] Since duplication of *phylae* is not otherwise found until the *demos* was suppressed in 91 B.C., I agree with Dinsmoor (p. 448) that Atene belonged at this time to Antiochis as well as to Demetrias.

[3] Or 6 if we restore Φρ[ε]α, which seems to accord better with the indications of the stone than ['E]ρο[ι]α (Kirchner).

[4] Reckoning, as is natural, from 201/0 B.C. as the starting point, the ninth archon-cycle began with 105/4. It might be thought that a new cycle was inaugurated in 157/6 B.C. (cf. *below*, pp. 146, 164), four years before the fourth

ments in the old one.[1] The evidence would be satisfied if, beginning at the time of its creation, Ptolemais were given an opportunity to draw lots for the polemarchship alone of the senior archonships; but it seems improbable that the new *phyle* was put thus at a disadvantage, especially since in this case the cycle of this office would end a year later than the cycles of the archonship and the kingship.

Since this alternate system of distributing offices among the tribes was used thus widely, we are not warranted in assuming without investigation that the official order was observed in each, or any, of the Tribal Cycles of priests of Asklepios between 322/1 and 277/6 B.C.; and, in fact, in the last cycle (288/7–277/6 B.C.) it was demonstrably not observed. The case of Phyleus of Eleusis is clear and unequivocal: in 286/5 B.C. Antigonis, not Hippothontis, is called for by the official order carried back from 276/5–157/6 B.C. Nor is this the only case. I yet adhere to the view expressed in a letter to Dinsmoor (p. 162, n. 4) that Onetor of Melite, of the *phyle* Demetrias, was priest of Asklepios, not, as there stated (my error), in the year the inventory IG^2 II 1534A was made, but in the year just completed,

[1] If the senior archonships were allotted each year and not, as assumed in the text, for a whole cycle at its beginning, Ptolemais could have been given its chance at all three offices in *ca.* 223 B.C. without disturbing the cycle. But the reasons which existed for deferring the sortition of the prytanies till the latest possible moment (*Athenian Secretaries*, pp. 20 ff.) did not apply in other cases. There was no danger that the assignment, long in advance, of the *phyle* to hold a magistracy in a particular year would lead to collusion in office; for, unlike the *prytaneis*, the individual who was to represent the *phyle* was not designated till the time arrived for his *phyle* to serve. Hence it is the more likely assumption that the allotment of *phylae* for the senior archonships was made at the beginning of the cycle, since nothing was to be gained by doing the allotting piecemeal.

CYCLES WITH ALLOTTED ORDER OF PHYLAE 55

i.e., 277/6 B.C., and that Philochares of Oa (Pandionis) was probably his close predecessor. Yet in 277/6 B.C. the official order demands Hippothontis, not Demetrias, and there is no place for a priest from Pandionis in his neighborhood.

The case for considering Onetor the priest of the year just ended when the inventory was ordered rests in part, but in part only, on the circumstance that he "appears both at the end of the main list and at the end (so far as preserved and perhaps the actual end) of the list of additional objects." The commissioners first catalogued the articles in the temple, area by area, adding for purposes of further identification the names of the priests in office when the votives were received. Then they entered three special categories of objects entitled respectively, "Silver articles in the possession of the priest," "(Other) articles in the possession of the priest," and "Articles which the god has in his hand." The final item in the last of these three groups runs, "also the articles dedicated during the priesthood of Onetor, namely, a gold *typidion*, weight . . ; ει . ιολ, *ca.* 28 letters." At this point the list of additional objects begins: "these articles, dedicated during his own term, Philochares of Oa, priest of Asklepios, handed over in addition - - - ; in the priesthood of Philip the priest of Asklepios handed over in addition these articles - - - ; these articles, dedicated under Charinos and Thrasybulos, the priest Onetor of Melite handed over in addition - - - ." What is the nature of these additional *traditiones*? To whom were they handed over? The answer is found in the phrases of the mutilated preamble to the inventory: "to hand over to the priest" (-s παραδοῦναι τῷ ἱερ[εῖ —], l. 6); "which he handed over to the priest for the archonship of Eubulos " (παρέδωκεν τῷ ἱερεῖ τῷ ἐπ' Ε[ὐβούλου ἄρχοντος], l. 8); "the other priests also are to be present" ([πα]ρεῖναι καὶ τοὺς ἄλλους [ἱερεῖς?], l. 9); "which he (the priest) has taken over weighed" (-s ἑστηκότα πα[ρ]είληφε[ν], l. 10). The implication is clearly that the objects (of gold and silver) which his predecessor handed over to the priest for the archonship of Eubulos he in turn was to hand over to the priest who followed him (Kolbe, *Hermes*, 1916, p. 545; Dinsmoor, p. 154), and that the commissioners, with the collaboration of the priest for Eubulos' year and of the other priests as well, were to make and publish on stone a record of the articles thus transferred "in order that the *traditio* might endure" ([ἵνα - - ἡ π]αράδοσις διαμένῃ). Priests handing over additional objects doubtless put them in the hands of the officiating priest or of the commissioners directly.

Put in terms of our findings, this means that Xenokritos of Aphidna, priest in P-'s archonship (276/5 B.C.) was the recipient of the articles catalogued, having received them from his predecessor, the priest of Eubulos' archonship (277/6 B.C.). What was the name of this priest?

As pointed out in Dinsmoor's work (p. 162), "in making the inventory the officials in charge listed the *exvotos* in the temple of Asklepius, not in the order of their dedication, but solely according to the position they occupied in the shrine." To this statement I should like to make an *addendum*, that it is true only of the main inventory and not of the record of additional articles. In their case the objects were grouped quite without reference to their position in the shrine. That

CYCLES WITH ALLOTTED ORDER OF *PHYLAE* 57

is to say, articles of this category are listed together notwithstanding that they were to be found in different parts of the temple area. Hence it would have been perverse for the commissioners not to arrange them in the chronological order of the priests who handed them over. In other words Onetor served last in this group of priests, the priest who handed over the additional objects dedicated in Philippos' year preceded him, not necessarily directly, and Philochares of Oa came earlier.

The view that Onetor was the priest whose term had just ended when the making of the inventory was ordered (the order was given in the second prytany of the year) is substantiated by his curious rôle in checking up the weights of the cult-apparatus in the possession of the priest. As we have seen, this is listed separately, ordinarily with no indication of the time at which it was received. Unlike the *ex-votos*, the articles of which it consisted, with the exception of two groups, are not attached to specific priesthoods. In this respect it is like "the silver vessels which the priests used" of *IG*² II 1534B, which, as we have seen, were entered in the annual register, not when received, but only when they went out of priestly use. At the time of the *exetasmos* in 276/5 B.C. the commissioners found, by the use of the scales, certain deficiencies in this equipment. Onetor is specially mentioned in connection with the ascertainment of others. The record runs: "three drinking cups, weight 144 drachmas; of these there is lacking to Onetor one drinking cup (τούτων ἐλλείπει παρ' Ὀνήτορι ποτήριον), weight 56 drachmas; the two that were put on the scales weighed 88 drachmas: ———, weight

328 drachmas; of this Onetor lacks from its weight
—— drachmas: a basket, weight 945 drachmas; from
this Onetor lacks the *anthemion*, weight 10 + drachmas."
Why should Onetor, and he alone, certify to the discrepancies if he was not responsible for the *paradosis*
which was being recorded? If the losses had come to
his attention during his tenure of office at an earlier
date, the past tense would have been called for. As we
have said, no other priest is concerned with the checking
up of the cult-apparatus. The uniqueness of Onetor's
rôle is intelligible when it is considered, that, if he served
in 277/6 B.C., the *exetasmos*, since it was made in the
second prytany of 276/5, was really an elaboration,
if not a part, of his *euthyna*.

In an earlier inventory of the Asklepieion (*IG*² II
1533, 341/0–336/5+ B.C.), in the section of the first
priest whose record is preserved (ll. 1 ff.), it is noted
of a crown "it does not exist" ([οὐ]κ ἔστιν); of ten
drachmas dedicated by Mnesarete "three are missing:
he said that Diokles of Myrrhinus (priest in 340/39)
was to return them; another lacks: Telesias (priest
in 336/5) has it." The record continues, "Onasos on
a *pinakis*, 12 drachmas; 4 are lacking: the sum lacking Polyxenos (priest in 339/8) paid back on his own
behalf." Further, "Minnion, 5 drachmas; the priest
Eunikides of Halai (who was in office in 341/0) said
that these were obsolete (παλαιάς)." Here the situation
is manifest. At the time of the ultimate *paradosis* (the
appearance of Diokles, Polyxenos, and Telesias shows
that the time is not the time of the making by Eunikides
of his original register) the commissioners found that
a crown and various drachmas dedicated in Eunikides'

CYCLES WITH ALLOTTED ORDER OF *PHYLAE* 59

year were missing. They called on him for an explanation. He gave it (ἔφη). The time of the discovery is the time of the making of the inventory; hence the present tense. The present tense is not used of a past transaction. It seems clear that it is not so used in Onetor's case. Onetor's concern for the condition of the cult-apparatus in 276/5 B.C. is intelligible only on the assumption that he was priest in 277/6 or that he was priest when this apparatus was first received; and in the latter case it would doubtless have been entered as dedicated (ἀνατεθέντα) during his priesthood. As it is, only two groups of articles in this category are so entered. At the end of the section entitled "These (other) articles are in the possession of the priest" appear "three jaspers, two crystal signets, a square cylinder entirely of crystal, an -*es* presented by Satyra, of which, according to the inscription, the fillet is of gold; it is, however, of silver plated with gold" — the whole group entered as dedicated in the priesthood of M-[of Kolo]nos?[1] And, as we have seen, at the end of the section entitled "These articles the god has in his hand" appear the gold *typidion* and one other article dedicated in the priesthood of Onetor. Obviously, the other cult-articles were not dedicated in his year.

We have, then, three priests with *demotika* for the cycle 288/7–277/6: Phyleus in 286/5, Onetor in 277/6, and Philochares in between; and they all belong to different *phylae*. If Nikonides of Phyla (Kekropis) is

---

[1] *IG*² II 1534A, l. 101. The stone reads: M .... νου. Restoring the only possible *demotikon* [ἐκ Κολω]ρου̂, ca. five spaces remain for the name of the priest. The alternative is a very long name. M[nesipolem]os and M[elesime]nes are probably too short.

dated correctly in this period (Dinsmoor, p. 164) — he can fall quite as well in one of the preceding cycles [1] — we have a fourth, and he is from yet another *phyle*. And perhaps M- [of Kolo]nos? (Aigeis) is to be added. This is not enough in itself to demonstrate that all the *phylae* were being given their turn by a process of allotment; but how explain otherwise the existence between 322/1 and 277/6 B.C. of cyclic continuity?

It now remains to determine, if possible, the point at which IG^2 II 1534A began. What remains of it contains the names of 19 + priests, one of whom may have been Phyleus (*above*, p. 45); and since a gap exists between frg. *ab* and frg. *c–k* on the reverse, a corresponding gap must have occurred at the same point on the obverse. From the number of annual sections missing on the reverse, allowing four lines per priest, we can compute that about 23 lines (.0078 cm. per line) are lost on the reverse [2] and about 18 (.0092 per line) on the obverse. The local disposition of the front inventory makes it impossible to compute how many priests are lost; for many priests are mentioned more than once, and most of the lines are incomplete. But since the

[1] The priests of Asklepios appearing in IG^2 II 1534A belong to the period, 300/299–277/6 B.C.: An-, Archestratos, Charinos, Diopheithes, Epikrates, Eudidaktos, Eumnestos, Lysias, M- [of Kolo]nos?, Onetor of Melite (277/6 B.C.), Ph-, Phaidrippos, Phanomachos, Philippos, Philochares of Oa, Philoktemon, Pythonikos, Theo-, Thrasyboulos. Besides Phyleus of Eleusis (286/5 B.C.) and Nikonides?, Demagenes (IG^1 II 1350), priest in the archonship of Nikias (296/5 B.C.; Dinsmoor, pp. 85, n. 1; 164), is to be added from other records.

[2] There is, accordingly, ample room for frg. *vo* (with 23 lines on the reverse, all defective) in the gap between frg. *ab* and frg. *c–k*. Mr. Dow informs me that the spacing of the letters shows that it belongs toward the top of the stone.

limits of IG^2 II 1534B are the ends of Tribal Cycles, we may assume that IG^2 II 1534A began as well as ended with a cycle, and since the two inventories occupied approximately the same space, we may infer that IG^2 II 1534A also covered two cycles. It should, therefore, have contained the records of 24 priests and have had its beginning in 300/299 B.C. At that time, we may now affirm, the practice existing as late as 304 B.C. of melting down yearly and at short intervals the silver votives in the Asklepieion for the making of vessels to be consigned to the keeping of the *tamiae* on the Acropolis was abandoned. It happens that 300/299 B.C. was the year of the *coup d'état* of Lachares who laid sacrilegious hands on the precious *ex-votos* on the Acropolis and converted them into money (*Class. Phil.*, 1929, pp. 1 ff.; *Treasurers of Athena*, pp. 126 f.). This was an appropriate epoch, surely, for inaugurating a new system, or, more accurately, reëstablishing the old system (IG^2 II 1532/3) of handling the votive offerings in the Asklepieion; [1] and, since the expropriation

[1] The entry of the articles in IG^2 II 1534A according to their local instead of their chronological disposition is not to be connected with the supplanting of rotation of the priests by allotment: the sequence of the priests could have been ascertained from the annual register of dedications, for which see Kirchner, IG^2 II 1534, note on p. 140. It is rather to be connected with the fact that in 276/5 B.C. the shrine contained no articles of silver and gold (apart from apparatus used in worship) not dedicated in the period covered by the scrutiny. Prior thereto such objects had been melted down annually and periodically. On the occasions of other scrutinies, when past accumulations were present in the temple as well as recent accessions, the annual registers of the priests were really what was being checked up, not the total contents of the shrine. There is no evidence that in 276/5 B.C. the objects inventoried were consigned to the melting pot: the purpose of the *exetasmos*, as stated in the prescript of IG^2 II 1534A, was to secure a permanent record of the *traditio*.

by the state of the temple properties required the issuance of an inventory,[1] 300/299 B.C. was the natural starting point of the next inventory.

On this construction of priestly cycles we have the anomaly that the official order was resumed in 276/5 B.C. with the eleventh *phyle*, Aiantis, instead of with the first, Antigonis. Two possible explanations need only to be stated to be rejected: (1) that owing to the so-called dictatorship of Olympiodoros in 294/2 B.C. Aiantis and Antiochis failed to get their turn in the preceding cycle, so that in compensation they were given the first positions when rotation in the official sequence was reintroduced. I am not satisfied with this way of escaping from our difficulty. There was a gap in these two years in the tribal sequence of the prytany-secretaries because under Olympiodoros the secretaries were replaced by registrars. It is unthinkable that the priests of Asklepios were replaced by other officials, or that there were no priests of Asklepios at all during these two years. Their suspension would involve the suspension of all the administrative services, and to me at least that is incredible. It is conceivable that the priest, like the archon, served for two consecutive years (cf. *below*, pp. 151 f.); but, if so, one *phyle* alone would have been pushed forward into the next cycle. (2) The other explanation is that the *phyle* to lead off in the new cycle was determined by sortition and the lot fell upon Aiantis. From the point of view of tribal representa-

---

[1] This may have listed cult-apparatus and μικρά left in the Asklepieion during the two cycles 322/1–313/2, and 312/1–301/0 B.C., thus filling the gap between IG^2 II 1532/3 (Dinsmoor, pp. 452 ff.) and IG^2 II 1534/5; but its authors were more probably the *tamiae* of Athena and its contents all the *ex-votos* of gold and silver in their custody.

tion it did not matter with which *phyle* the rotation in the fixed order began: every *phyle* would hold the priesthood between 288/7 and 277/6 and between 276/5 and 265/4 B.C. Perhaps it was only in the course of 276/5 B.C. (when Aiantis had already received the priesthood by allotment), conceivably at the time of the *exetasmos* in the second prytany, that the decision to reëstablish the official order was taken. In favor of this hypothesis is the fact that when in 356/5 B.C. the official order was first introduced for the prytany-secretaries (and doubtless also for the priests of Asklepios) the cycle began, not with Erechtheis, but with Kekropis, i.e., with the *phyle* allotted to hold the office in that year. The decision to use the fixed sequence for the secretaries of the *tamiae* of Athena was made, seemingly, at the same time, i.e., in 356, to become operative with Leontis in 355/4 B.C. (*Treasurers of Athena*, pp. 143 f.). Against this hypothesis is the consideration that, as indeed the choice of Leontis in the case of the secretary of the *tamiae* shows, the *introduction* of a cyclic system of rotation permitted the free use of the lot to determine the tribal leader while its resumption did not. This explanation is also inadequate in that sortition pure and simple leaves unexplained the frequency with which Aiantis inaugurated Tribal Cycles (see *below*, pp. 78 ff.).

There are, moreover, two acceptable explanations of the seeming anomaly, one consonant with each of the methods suggested above (p. 47) for preserving cyclic continuity between 356/5–322/1 B.C. and 276/5. The first of these has been stated already: it assumes rotation in the official order between 307/6 B.C. (Aigeis) and 289/8 B.C. (Hippothontis) and one cycle only

(288/7–277/6 B.C.) of rotation by allotment. As this is perhaps the preferable explanation, it has been utilized in constructing Table II (pp. 22 f.). An innovation in 288 B.C. is well motivated by the new democratic regime then established. The other explanation accords with cycles of allotted order between 322/1 and 276/5 B.C. It capitalizes the coincidence that when in 306/5 B.C., after the start with Aigeis in 307/6 had been vitiated by the transfer of Diomeia to Demetrias, the secretary-cycle was reëstablished, it also began with Aiantis (Dinsmoor, pp. 36, 56; cf. also p. 450 and n. 3).[1] The suggestion is that in 276 B.C. the precedent of 306 B.C. was followed (see *below*, pp. 78 ff.).

[1] Between 307/6 and 304/3 B.C. four *phylae* served in the following order II, XI, 12, I. Diomeia, which furnished the secretary in 307/6, was transferred in the course of the year from Aigeis to Demetrias, and in compensation, Demetrias was not given the secretariat in 303/2 B.C. after Antigonis (Dinsmoor, pp. 36 f.). The premature turn of Demetrias being the result of events that were unforeseen at the opening of 307/6, we have to explain the jump from Aigeis to Aiantis at the end of this year; and the best explanation is that adopted by Dinsmoor (pp. 38, 56), viz., that the official order was introduced anew with the eleventh *phyle* (Aiantis) in 306/5 B.C. The choice of Aigeis in 307/6 B.C. was regular: the secretary-cycle had ended in 322/1 B.C., on the first appointment of registrars, with Erechtheis. The four secretaries (with *demotika*) now assigned to 318/7–308/7 B.C., Thersippos of Acharnae (IG^2 II 448, 318/7 B.C.), — of Lamptrai (IG^2 II 545, after 318/7 B.C.), — of Hagnus (IG^2 II 452, 313/2 B.C.; Dinsmoor, p. 376), and — of Rhamnus (IG^2 II 454, 308/7 B.C.), came from different *phylae* (VI, I, V, IX). They can have succeeded in an allotted order, not seemingly in the official order. A new cycle was due to begin in 308/7 B.C., and curiously enough (cf. pp. 78 ff.) it began with Aiantis, if IG^2 II 454 is dated correctly.

We observe further that, if the cycle of the priests of Artemis Kalliste began (i.e., was resumed) in 307/6 B.C. with Aigeis, and jumped, like that of the prytany-secretary, to Demetrias in the course of the year, the priests for the years 237/6 and 236/5 B.C. (IG^2 II 1297, 788; cf. *Klio*, 1907, p. 213; Dinsmoor, pp. 103 f.) fall in proper cyclic relation. The priest for 307/6 may have belonged to Diomeia.

V. Stability of Priestly Cycles of Asklepios

On the construction thus worked out we observe that whereas the secretarial cycle was broken by the degradation of the office of prytany-secretary in 321/0–319/8 B.C. (*Athenian Secretaries*, p. 42; Brillant, *Les secrétaires athéniens*, pp. 60, 88 ff.; Dinsmoor, pp. 16 ff.), suspended by its abolition in 294/2 B.C. (Dinsmoor, *loc. cit.*), and broken again in 263/2 B.C. after the capture of Athens by Antigonus Gonatas, the priestly cycle (in official or, as in 288/7–277/6 B.C., allotted order) was maintained without interruption, unless it be for the interval between 321/0 and 308/7 B.C. (which, as we have seen, may have been treated as outside the *cadres* altogether), from the first introduction of the system (356/5? B.C.) to the end of the third century and beyond. It may be thought that this conclusion is deceptive; that it results from the circumstance that we lack the data (names and dates of priests) the possession of which would enable us, perhaps, to establish the existence of breaks. But there is a consideration which inclines us to the opinion that the greater stability of the priestly cycle corresponds with realities. The priesthood was a non-political office. In this respect it approximated rather the secretariat of the *tamiae* than the prytany-secretariat, which was connected intimately with the conduct of political affairs by the Council and *demos*, and was consequently more subject to political interference. I have commented elsewhere (*Treasurers of Athena*, pp. 141, 151 ff.) on the tenacity with which the Athenians preserved the Tribal Cycles in the case of the secretaries of the *tamiae* of Athena. Between their definite inauguration in 411 B.C. and the disappearance of the office in our records the cycles were maintained steadfastly despite frequent revolutions and the integration (twice repeated) and disintegration of the office of the secretaries' principals with the board of *tamiae* of the Other Gods. The priesthood of Asklepios was even less exposed to deviations from routine than the secretariat of the *tamiae*. Hence on a priori grounds we are prepared for the prolonged stability of the priestly cycle.

VI. Philippos, Kimon, Xenophon, Peithidemos

Mr. Dow reports that the letters in line two of IG^2 II 703 which Wilhelm (add., p. 665) read as HI might be NT, thus permitting the restoration ['A]ντ[ιοχίδος], and allowing us to complete the lines uniformly with 31 letters; but, since traces of a cross-bar are discernible in the first letter and traces of two parallel uprights in the second, he concedes a greater degree of probability to Wilhelm's reading of the first letter. The second he reads as M, thus requiring us to restore the prytany as [Δ]ημ[ητριάδος]. For the secretary from Antiochis (L . . on, son of Miltiades, of Alopeke) five years are open: 292/1 (Philippos), 280/79 (Gorgias?), 262/1 (Arrheneides), 250/49, and 238/7 (Lysias). We do not have the divisions of the lines in IG^2 II 703. Hence we turn to IG^2 II 702, a decree of the same year, for a computation of the number of spaces occupied by the archon's name. Unfortunately this inscription was not written *stoichedon*. Kirchner estimates that the name occupied *ca.* seven spaces in the genitive. A symmetrical disposition of the text and superscription of IG^2 II

703 seems to demand an archon-name with eight letters as a minimum.[1]

The year was an intercalary year, with an irregular intercalation of one of the first four months (Kirchner, note). Dinsmoor (pp. 395 ff.), assuming a stonecutter's error in order to get rid of the irregularity, concludes, none the less, that it was intercalary. This disposes of Lysias. Since the year of his predecessor was intercalary, his year must have been ordinary. According to Scheme A, Table II, 250/49 B.C. must also have been ordinary, since otherwise we should have a sequence of two intercalary or three ordinary years.[2] The year of Philippos and 280/79 and 262/1 B.C. remain. Philippos' year was seemingly intercalary, 280/79 was preferably ordinary (see Table II). 262/1 was certainly ordinary (Dinsmoor, p. 166). Dinsmoor (pp. 73 f.) assigns IG^2 II 796/7 (with . . . . . . os, son of Lykos, of Alopeke (XII) as secretary, and an archon whose name had nine letters in the genitive) to 280/79; but relying on Kirchner's report as to the letter-forms (*med. s.* III), I have assigned this pair of decrees to 250/49 B.C.

---

[1] Mr. Dow has noted a bit of the moulding directly above the nu of the superscription, which was accordingly written, in large deep letters, across the top of the stone — thus, [Μυρλε] *vac. ca.* .113 cm. ανω[ν] (cf. IG^2 II 63). Careful measurements of the stone show that, if the text was situated symmetrically with the superscription, the archon-name must have had eight or more spaces. With an archon-name of six letters the lines must have begun *ca.* .010⅔ cm. to the right of the initial letter (mu) of the superscription and ended .030¼ cm. to the right of the final nu, even if we assume, as is probable, that the five letters Μυρλε occupied the same space (.129 cm.) as the four letters ανων. With Wilhelm's reading line two or three had 32 letters. Perhaps the iota of [Δ]ημ[ητριάδος was crowded in at the end of line two, thus preserving syllabification.

[2] According to Scheme B, Table II, 250/49 B.C. is indeterminate.

(Kydenor's year, according to Scheme A, Table II). The choice between 292/1 and 280/79 can also be made on other grounds. The chairman of the *proedri* in IG^2 II 702 was Demetrios, son of Demetrios, of Phaleron. On the assumption that this was the grandson (see *below*, pp. 84 f.) of the famous Demetrius, Dinsmoor (p. 170) dates IG^2 II 702/3 after the capture of Athens in 263/2 B.C. (specifically in 256/5 B.C.). But he can have been equally well the son of the regent of 317/07 B.C. And this, I believe, is who he was. The year (inserting the archon-name Philippos in IG^2 II 702/3) was the one in the course of which Poliorcetes restored the exiles banished after the downfall of the regent in 307 B.C. (Dionys. Hal., *de Dinarcho*, 2 f., 4, 9). The son of the regent was, doubtless, one of their number. It was fitting that the exiles should be given forthwith a share in the government, since presumably it was for this purpose that they were recalled. But even if the recall had been issued in the first days of the year, a week or so must have elapsed before they were back in Athens. With this situation I should connect the calendar confusion attested by IG^2 II 702/3. One of the first four months of the year was intercalated irregularly. It can have been Hekatombaion. Assigning days to the prytanies as follows: to I 29, to II–V 32, to VI–VII 33, to VIII 34, to IX–XI 32, and to XII 31, we satisfy the equations of the two decrees, that Maimakterion 21 equal prytany VI, 11, and Elaphebolion 22 equal prytany IX, 30, and at the same time allow an opportunity at the beginning of Hekatombaion II for the supplanting by secondary elections of some officials to make place for exiles. It was then, on this hypothesis, that Demetrios, son of Demetrios, of Phaleron entered the Council. In any event, it is highly improbable that a son of the regent should have been active in political life in 280/79 B.C. It was the time when the fortunes of Antigonus were at their lowest ebb.

The regime of 294/2 B.C. may have had "oligarchic" traditions: the reappearance of *anagrapheis* implies thus much; but it must also have had nationalistic tendencies: otherwise the participation in it of Olympiodoros is unintelligible. From its autonomistic attitude, as well as because of its usurpation of power for a second year, Poliorcetes can have decided to dilute it with men whose Macedonian leanings were now more assuring to him than their former support of Kassander, then his rival, now his predecessor, was prejudicial. After recalling them he could count on their devotion to his own person.

Despite the seemingly cogent argumentation of Dinsmoor (pp. 70 f.) for dating Kimon as late as 282/1 B.C. I think that 289/8 B.C. must still be considered as a possibility for him. The question hinges on the construction of IG^2 II 682, ll. 24 ff.: καὶ ἐπὶ τὴν χώραν χειροτονηθεὶς (Φαῖδρος) πλεονάκις καὶ ἐπὶ τοὺς ξένους γενόμενος τρὶς τὴν πᾶσαν ἐποήσατο σπουδήν, ὅπως ἂν οἱ στρατιῶται ὡς ἄριστα κατασκευασάμενοι παρέχωνται τὰς χρείας τῶι δήμωι. If, as Dinsmoor assumes, the commands ἐπὶ τὴν χώραν and ἐπὶ τοὺς ξένους were held consecutively, Kimon (under whom Phaidros was hoplite-general) cannot have followed Nikias, 296/5 B.C. (under whom he was elected general ἐπὶ τὴν παρασκευὴν δίς) by so short an interval as six years; but there are certain considerations which oppose the idea of consecutive tenures of these charges. It is to be observed that the two are treated as one in the predication of services. Moreover, as I have pointed out already (*Class. Phil.*, 1906, p. 310; *Klio*, 1909, p. 317), there is no evidence that Athens ever had a *strategia ἐπὶ τοὺς ξένους*. Such an office is not implied in *Pap. Oxy.*, XVII, 2082, frg. 1. Lachares, one of the *strategi*, is there defined as ὁ τῶν ξένων ἡγούμενος. On other occasions the ξένοι are under the general ἐπὶ τὴν χώραν or, when this command was divided, under the general ἐπ' Ἐλευσῖνος or the general ἐπὶ τὴν παραλίαν. There is a subordinate *hegemon* or *xenagos* (*IG*² II 1313) in charge of the detachments of ξένοι, regularly a mercenary. Taking the text and the military institutions into account, I think it likely that Phaidros was elected πλεονάκις to the generalship ἐπὶ τὴν χώραν in the interval between Nikias and Kimon, and as such came to command (γενόμενος ἐπί) the ξένοι on three occasions. Assuming the interval in question to be one of six years, the ξένοι can be assumed to have been under the command of the hoplite-general on the other three occasions (*IG*² II 1300). The point is that by dating Kimon in 289/8 B.C. we are in a position to explain the crisis (καιρῶν δυσκόλων), involving the Macedonian king, — the excisions in *IG*² II 682 show this, — in which Phaidros as hoplite-general "preserved peace in the country, - - was responsible for harvesting the grain and other crops, - - and handed over the state free and democratic and the laws in full vigor to those who succeeded him." The crisis was the revolt from Demetrius and the war which ensued. It is intelligible that the attitude of the hoplite-general for 289/8 B.C., a man theretofore and later of the Macedonian party in Athens, had much to do with making this abrupt transition from the regime established by Demetrius in 292/1 B.C. to the popular nationalist regime of 288/7 B.C. an orderly one. With Dinsmoor's date for Kimon (282/1 B.C.) we have to invent a crisis to explain Phaidros' activity. Any desired archon-name of the required length (seven letters in the genitive) can be restored in *IG*² II 670A in place of Kimon.

Phaidros reappears in the archonship of Xenophon. In the famous honorary decree devoted to his services, which we now know to have been passed after 263/2 B.C., he is said to have been "elected by the people hoplite-general for Xenophon's year first (πρῶτος)." The context was excised in 200 B.C., so that the "first" remains an enigma. Dinsmoor, whose date for Xenophon (274/3 B.C.) seems practically certain, says (p. 77), "this probably means that there were two hoplite generals in that year, and, since there could not have been two hoplite generals simultaneously, it would seem that there was a political change in the course of the year, Phaidros being general in the first part and replaced before the conclusion of his term." But if there were two hoplite-generals, there were probably two Councils also, as in 296/5 B.C. That, however, *IG*² II 704 (for the date of which see *below*, p. 77, n. 1) excludes. *IG*² II 477, which Dinsmoor dates in 274/3 B.C., would furnish no ground for inferring a change of political regime in the course of its year. In regard to "first" it would probably be prudent to imitate the restraint of Dittenberger (*Syll.*³, 409, n. 17): *Quo haec vox spectet, obscurum est, nisi quod Phaedrus primus post nescio quam rerum publicarum mutationem praetor creatus esse dicitur.* But ἐς Τροίαν πειρώμενοι ἦνθον 'Αχαιοί, "it was by dint of trying that the

Achaeans got into Troy." The lengthy excisions before and after the sentence in question show that allusions were made to Antigonus which seemed reprehensible in 200 B.C. The occurrence in reference to which, after 263/2 B.C., the generalship of Phaidros was defined as "first" must have been a memorable one. I conjecture that it was the loss of the Piraeus. It seems clear that at the time of the ransom of Mithres by Epicurus, Olympiodoros being general in Athens (281–0 B.C.), Antigonus possessed the Piraeus (*Pap. Herc.*, no. 1418, col. xxxiii)[1] and equally clear that it was in his hands in 274/3 B.C. (*Diog. Laert.*, II, 127; Beloch, *Griech. Gesch.*, IV 2, p. 608; Dinsmoor, p. 117). Accordingly, he must have lost it after 281–0 and recovered it in or before 274/3 B.C. Its loss is unthinkable after his accession to the throne of Macedon in 277 B.C. Hence, as Segre argues (*Annuario del R. Liceo Dante Alighieri di Bressanone*, 1928/9, pp. 1 ff.), the capture of the Piraeus, which Pausanias (I, 26, 3) terms the "greatest exploit" of Olympiodoros, was achieved between 281 and 277 B.C.;[2] and within these limits the year in which Antigonus' fortunes were at their lowest ebb (280/79 B.C.) is the one in which we should naturally place its loss (*Justin*, XXIV,

[1] Vogliano, *Riv. di Fil.*, 1926, p. 322; 1927, pp. 501 ff.; cf. Beloch, *idem*, 1926, pp. 331 ff.; De Sanctis, *idem*, 1927, pp. 491 ff.

[2] As to the reality of this exploit opinions notoriously differ; rather, have differed. It is now generally recognized that our ignorance of the history of the epoch is too great to justify us in rejecting Pausanias' explicit statement. As to the time of the recovery opinions still differ. Tarn (*CAH*, VII, p. 89) decided in favor of 285 B.C., Beloch (*Griech. Gesch.*, IV 2, pp. 607 ff.) in favor of 274/2. I should like to withdraw the suggestion I have made (*Class. Phil.*, 1929, p. 4, n. 1) that it was 301/0 B.C. Dinsmoor does not express himself clearly on the point, but he dates in 274 B.C. an epoch of Macedonian influence in Athens.

1; Tarn, *CAH*, VII, pp. 99 f.). Its recovery by him is unchronicled. It is unthinkable before he had established himself firmly in Macedon, and 275/4 must be the approximate time. If it is to this that "first" harks back its recovery is dated therewith in 275/4 B.C. precisely. It is intelligible that Antigonus, then master of the resources of Macedon and again powerful in Greece, forced Athens, with nobody to aid her,[1] to surrender to him the Piraeus. The Piraeus was probably the price paid by Athens for peace and liberty. In the moment when the danger thickened in the north the Athenians turned to Phaidros and his party for counsel and help. His son Thymochares was elected *agonothetes* for 277/6 B.C. He himself became hoplite-general in 274/3. But this was the end of his political career. On the advent of Pyrrhus in Greece the nationalists regained the ascendancy (Tarn, *JHS*, 1920, pp. 143 ff.); and on his death (272 B.C.) they linked themselves to Ptolemy, whom the end of the First Syrian War (271 B.C.) freed for activity in Greece. They had to sustain an attack from Antigonus in 269/8 B.C. (*IG*^{2} II 665–7). Dinsmoor (p. 81) dates the archon Peithidemos in 270/69 B.C., and argues for placing thus early the alliance of Athens with Sparta and Ptolemy which led to the Chremonidean War (cf., however, *Class. Rev.*, 1932, p. 124). What weighs chiefly in its favor is the reference in *IG*^{2} II 687, l. 16 (cf. add.) to the "policy of the sister" of Philadelphus, who died on July 9th, 270 B.C. But the works of Arsinoe lived after her. It was not till 259 B.C. that her son (?) ceased to be co-regent with her

---

[1] Pyrrhus was in Italy, Ptolemy and Antiochus engaged in the First Syrian War.

brother-husband. It is possible that the Athenians were driven by the hostilities of 269/8 B.C. into taking the fatal plunge. And since 267/6 B.C. is equally available for Peithidemos the question is not yet closed (see, however, *above*, p. 38). From IG^2 II 665, ll. 13 ff. we may infer either that there was a pause in the war before the third prytany of 268/7 B.C. or that this war was then over.

If the capture of the Piraeus by Olympiodoros is correctly dated in 280/79 B.C., the action of Demochares of Leukonoe in securing the vote of honors and a bronze statue for Demosthenes in the archonship of Gorgias (280/79 B.C.) ([Plut.], *Lives of the Ten Orators*, 847d, 850 f.) acquires an appropriate historical setting. Similarly the honors voted by the Athenians in 271/0 B.C. to Demochares, Demosthenes' nephew ([Plut.], *op. cit.*, 847d, 851d), take on a new significance when the decision to reopen the struggle with Macedon is dated, as by Dinsmoor, in the second prytany of 270/69 B.C. At this time the memories of the Athenians were Demosthenic. Their spirit was anti-Macedonian; but pending the conclusion of the negotiations with Sparta and Egypt Athens was careful to avoid giving offense to Antigonus (*Hell. Ath.*, p. 173). On the whole, I am inclined to date Peithidemos in 270/69 B.C. The war which ended with the fall of Athens in 263/2 B.C. is said to have lasted a "very long time." [1]

---

[1] The war was in progress in 269/8 B.C. Interrupted in 268/7, it was resumed in 266, and in 265 Areus was defeated and slain. The mutiny of the Gauls and the attack of Alexander of Epirus on Macedon gave Athens respites, which Patroklos doubtless used to introduce supplies, In the late autumn of 263 or the early spring of 262 the city fell. The chronology of the struggle *can* be worked out on the assumption that the treaty from which it developed was struck in August, 270.

VII. Tribal Cycles and Archons during the Darkest Age

We note, first of all, that Diomedon is fixed in 253/2 B.C. by a double bond, (1) by carrying back the secretary-cycles from 221/0 B.C. (Thrasyphon archon, Lower Paiania (V) furnishing the secretary), and (2) by the carrying forward of the priestly cycles of Asklepios from 322/1 B.C. In other words, the two cycles vouch for each other.

It is a necessary consequence that there was a break in the secretary-cycle at or near the capture of Athens by Antigonus. Pivoted on Diomedon in 253/2 B.C., this cycle demands that Antigonis hold the secretaryship in 261/0 B.C.[1] It is plausible that the Athenians should have honored Antigonus by giving the *phyle* which bore his family name the first place in the secretary-cycle when this was resumed after the break. But why should the break have occurred in 261 B.C.? The natural place for the break is in 263/2 B.C., at the time when the nationalist officials were replaced by supporters of the conqueror. Something, however, can be said for its postponement till 261 B.C. With 261/0 B.C. a new Metonic Cycle was inaugurated. In the archonship of Thrasynon at Delos (261 B.C., Durrbach; 260

---

[1] Assuming with Dinsmoor (pp. 107 ff.) that Antigonus Gonatas died in the spring of 240 B.C., Ekphantos may have been archon as early as 237/6 B.C. without doing violence to the career of Apollonios (*above*, pp. 13 ff.). With this date as a pivot we reach 262/1 B.C. for Antigonis; but this would involve the difficulty that Diomedon would have to fall in 254/3 B.C., which the priestly cycles of Asklepios pivoting on 322/1 B.C. do not permit. Equally serious is the fact that we should have to postulate a break of one *phyle* in the secretary-cycle between 237/6 B.C. and 221/0 (Thrasyphon).

B.C., Dinsmoor,[1] p. 503) the word "peace" is inserted extraordinarily in the formula which follows the name of the archon in the archon's accounts (ὑγίεια εἰρήνη πλοῦτος ἐγένετο, *IG* XI 2, 114, cf. *below*, p. 115 for a similar entry). This has been interpreted by Tarn (cf. *CAH*, VII, p. 708, n. 1) and others (Otto, *Philologus*, 86, 1931, pp. 416 ff.) as signifying that in this year the overlord of Delos concluded "peace." The parties who come primarily in question are Antigonus and Ptolemy (cf. *below*, p. 131, n. 1). We can, therefore, assume that it was in 261 B.C. that the war between the two monarchs, of which the Chremonidean War and the capture of Athens were incidents, came to a close. It may have been, not their own defeat, but the issue of the general war, leaving Athens to Antigonus, which the Athenians chose to signalize by giving the place of honor to Antigonis in 261/0 B.C. Moreover, there was possibly an interim regime of some sort in Athens between its capture and 261 B.C.[2] The second phrase of

[1] In order to find room for all the Delian archon-names which have reached us, Dinsmoor, on placing the main body of archons one year later than Durrbach to meet the requirements of his calendar-cycle of 16 years, has to assume that two archons served in the one year, 210 B.C. (p. 502). It seems clear that the Greeks, like the Romans, named the year from the first eponymous official alone when death or something similar made a *suffectus* necessary. Otherwise more than one name must have appeared attached to individual years with some frequency in the long lists of Athenian, Delian, and Delphian archons and of Milesian *aesymnetae* which have reached us. Exceptions *did* occur, however. In 411/0 B.C. both Mnasilochos and Theopompos were eponymous at Athens, and in 124/3 B.C. both Nikias and Isigenes. We know no reason for the latter of these two exceptions. Again in 90–100 A.D. (*IG*² II 1759) Philopappos and Lailianos were archons in the same year.

[2] In the decree of Arrheneides' year preserved in Diogenes Laertius (VII, 10) the secretary appears as usual. As is the case sporadically throughout this entire century, he is entitled γραμματεὺς τοῦ δήμου (cf. *below*, p. 160, n. 1).

CYCLES AND ARCHONS DURING DARKEST AGE 77

Apollodoros' statement ([καὶ τὰς] ἀρχὰς [ἀνῃρῆσθ]αι καὶ πᾶν ἐν[ὶ] βουλεύ[ειν? ἐφ]εῖσθαι) suggests a Macedonian regency. It can be thought that this ended with the "peace."[1]

[1] The dating of IG^2 II 704 in 262/1 B.C. (Dinsmoor, p. 167) would be quite uncertain even if we were sure that Leontis held the secretaryship in that year: it belongs nicely in the archonship of Xenophon, 274/3 B.C., where I have placed it in Table II, dislodging IG^2 II 477. IG^2 II 477 = SEG, III, 89 (Wilhelm, *Attische Urkunden*, III, pp. 39 ff.) has a secretary from the deme Potamos and an archon whose name had *ca.* twelve letters in the genitive. Potamos belonged to both Leontis (VI) and Antigonis (I). According to Scheme A, Table II, no place is available for a secretary from Leontis and an archon with a name thus long; according to Scheme B, 232/1 B.C. (archon Eurykleides) is open, but excluded by the reference to King Antigonus. For a secretary from Antigonis the possibilities are 279/8 (archon Anaxikrates), 267/6, and 261/0 (archon Sosistratos?). 279/8 is excluded because the name of the secretary contained *ca.* 27 letters instead of 21 (Dinsmoor, p. 78). 267/6 is also excluded because the contents of IG^2 II 477 show that it cannot have been passed after IG^2 II 687 so long as the Chremonidean War lasted (IG^2 II 687 was passed during the second prytany, IG^2 II 477 during the fifth). 261/0 alone remains. With this date, in a decree passed on the 2d of Posideon, 261/0 B.C., we have an interesting reference to the recent dispatch of envoys by the Athenians to ... aia (Nikaia?) to negotiate for the "renewal? of friendship [and peace] with King Antigonus." I assume that they took part in the pourparlers which eventuated in the "peace" of 261 B.C., and secured the withdrawal of the military "monarch" to whom, according to Apollodoros, Antigonus had given "the full power of decision" in 263/2 B.C. In 263/2 B.C. Athens had had to surrender unconditionally (*Hell. Ath.*, p. 182, n. 1). The decree in honor of Zenon, recently deceased, which is dated on Maimakterion 21st, 262/1 B.C., was passed at the king's request (*Diog. Laert.*, VII, 15). Thrason of Anakaia, who made the motion, received the commission to do so while present as an ambassador of Athens at the court. He can have been one of the envoys of IG^2 II 477. Sosistratos is of the right length for the lacuna in line one.

The year of IG^2 II 477 is commonly taken to be intercalary; but, as Dinsmoor notes (p. 394, n. 1), it can be regarded as ordinary by restoring [δευτέρα]ι, in line five and assuming that in this year the first group of prytanies had 30 days each. It was not unusual to have the first five or six prytanies uniform and different in length from the rest (IG^2 II 499, 657); and in 306/5 B.C., for example, the first six had 30 days each (IG^2 II 470). In

None the less, it is undeniable that 263/2 B.C. is the more natural point for the break. We have already seen that it was then that the series of archon-cycles existent in 228/7 B.C. was inaugurated (*above*, p. 52); and it was then that in the course of the year a new priest of Asklepios supplanted his nationalist predecessor. We shall do well, I think, to recognize that it was then that the new secretary-cycle began. It, accordingly, began with Aiantis.[1] So long as the beginning of a tribal series in official order with this *phyle* was an isolated occurrence there was nothing to be said in its favor. But we have now discovered that possibly in 308/7 and certainly in 306/5 B.C. the secretary-cycle was inaugurated with Aiantis (*above*, p. 64, n. 1; cf. p. 22), and that in 276/5 B.C. the priestly cycle of Asklepios recognized thereafter was also inaugurated with this *phyle* (*above*, pp. 62 ff.); and we shall see later (*below*, pp. 171 ff.) that in 145/4 B.C. Aiantis was selected out of turn to begin this same priestly cycle when the official order, which had been supplanted between 157/6 and 146/5 B.C. by a cycle of allotted order of *phylae*, was resumed. The fact that Aiantis was accorded a privileged position among the Attic *phylae* was already noted and discussed by Plutarch.[2] The question brought before a

---

the fourth century the norm was for the first four prytanies to have 36 days and the last six to have 35 (Arist., *Ath. Pol.*, 43, 2). Dinsmoor's objection that δευτέραι is too long for the space is invalid. On the contrary it is precisely right, giving a line of 26 letters, like lines two, four, and six (*SEG*, III, 89). I take the year of IG^2 II 477 to be ordinary.

[1] It was perhaps a studied coincidence that on beginning with Aiantis in 263/2 B.C. Antigonis fell in 261/0, the opening year of the Metonic Cycle (cf. *below*, p. 175, n. 2).

[2] Of the 64 eponymous archons whose *phylae* are known between 116/7

group assembled ostensibly in Athens to celebrate the choregic victory of a certain Sarapion gained when King Philopappos was *agonothetes* (Plut., *Quaest. Conviv.* I, 10) was formulated thus: Διὰ τί τῆς Αἰαντίδος φυλῆς 'Αθήνησιν οὐδέποτε τὸν χορὸν ἔκρινον ὕστατον. As authority for the reality of the privilege Plutarch cites Neanthes of Cyzicus. The answers given to the question by the assembled guests were as follows: Harmodios and Aristogeiton belonged to Aphidna, an Aiantid deme; so did the polemarch Kallimachos. Marathon was a deme of Aiantis. Aiantis had the place of honor at the extreme right of the line in the famous battle; it was also the prytanizing *phyle* when the march out from the city was decided upon. Aiantis distinguished itself in the battle of Plataea, sustained all (?) the casualties (Kleidemos), and was given the privilege of conducting to Cithaeron the thank offerings of the city to the Sphragitic Nymphs (cf. Plut., *Aristid.*, 19, 4 f.). As Plutarch himself remarks, they do not seem convincing: other *phylae* could adduce counterbalancing claims. Toeppfer (*PW*, I 1, pp. 929 f.) writes: Die Aiantis nahm unter den 10 attischen Phylen eine bevorzugte Stellung ein, was mit dem Bestreben der Athener zusammenhängt, die Insel Salamis, deren Heros Aias war, möglichst eng und dauernd mit Attika zu verknüpfen. The position of Aiantis was certainly peculiar, and recognized as such (*Herod.*, V, 66), in that it alone of the Kleisthenian *phylae* had a non-Attic, i.e., Salaminian, hero as

---

and 222/3 A.D. 22 belonged to Aiantis (count by Mr. James Notopoulos on the basis of Graindor, *Chronologie des archontes athéniens sous l'Empire*, Mem. de l' Acad. royale de Belgique, Classe des Lettres, 8, 1922, pp. 291 ff., and of Kirchner, IG^2 II et III, II^2, pp. 789 ff.).

eponymus; but the Athenians settled on Salamis belonged probably to all the Attic *phylae*, certainly not to Aiantis exclusively (IG^2 II 1225–1228). As confirmatory of the special consideration shown Aiantis, I note that it was the only *phyle* not dismembered by surrendering demes for the creation in 307/6 B.C. of Antigonis and Demetrias (Dinsmoor, p. 450).[1] It was the first *phyle*, numbering from the right, in the battle line at Marathon (Busolt, *Griech. Gesch.*, II, p. 589, n. 4); it had a post of special danger at Plataea. It is, I think, conceivable that the "men of Ajax" always formed the first regiment, on the extreme right, in the place of honor, in the Athenian citizen army. Manifestly it was an alternate for Erechtheis or Antigonis as coryphaeus in the rotating series of *phylae* after the epoch of Demetrius of Phaleron, who belonged to this *phyle* and instituted a lasting reform of the tribal competitions at festivals (*Hell. Ath.*, p. 55). Of course, the prerogative of Aiantis may be derived wholly from the issue of sortition in 306 B.C.

As Dinsmoor (p. 173), following Johnson (*AJP*, 1913, p. 404; *Class. Phil.*, 1914, p. 433), has pointed out Pheidostratos is the only archon-name long enough to fill the requirements of IG^2 II 734. This gives a secretary from Ikaria (I or IV); and since Pheidostratos' successor, Antimachos (Dinsmoor, p. 172), has a secretary from Myrrhinus (V), we have now the assurance that the Tribal Cycles in the official order were maintained for the prytany-secretaries, as well as for the priests of Asklepios, during the period (263/2–256/5

---

[1] This is all the more notable in that it occurred just prior to the first well-attested instance of the "privilege" of Aiantis, that of 306 B.C.

B.C.) when Antigonus held Athens by a garrison in the Museum.

In Table II our attention is attracted by the curious names borne by the archons between 261/0 B.C. and 256/5: Sosistratos?, Philostratos, Phanostratos, Pheidostratos, Antimachos, and Kleomachos. The assignment of Sosistratos to 261/0 B.C. is conjectural. In Polystratos' year a commission of Thracians in Athens had been selected to construct there a *hieron* of Bendis,[1] and they had opened negotiations on behalf of the urban *orgeones* for whom they acted, to secure for their representatives participation on equal terms with the officials of the mother society of Thracian *orgeones* of

---

[1] Now that three *stelae* with decrees of *thiasotai* of Bendis have been found at Salamis (IG^2 II 1317, 1317b add.; *SEG*, II, 10), it is unlikely that they were all carried over from the Piraeus, as Wilhelm (*Oester. Jahresh.*, V, 1902, p. 131) suggested when we had to deal with one *stele* alone. None of these decrees emanated, however, from Thracians. There was also an association of Athenian *orgeones* in the Piraeus for the worship of Bendis (Plato, *Rep.*, I, 1, p. 327). The meetings of this society were fixed by law (IG^2 II 1361) on the 2d day of the month; those of the Thracians were held on the 8th (IG^2 II 1283, 1284). The latter conferred a crown of oak leaves (IG^2 II 1284, l. 29): the former conferred a crown of olive (IG^2 II 1324, l. 19; cf. Wilhelm, *loc. cit.*, p. 132; Kirchner, IG^2 II 1361, note). Since the meetings of the society at Salamis were held on the 2d of the month (Skirophorion, i.e., as soon as possible after the Bendideia, which were celebrated on Thargelion 19th; Schol. Plato, *Rep.*, p. 327a), and the crown conferred was of olive (IG^2 II 1317, 1317b add.; *SEG*, II, 10), it appears that this association was an offshoot of the Athenian *orgeones* in the Piraeus. Its members, however, were *thiasotai*, not *orgeones*. This implies, doubtless, that they were neither Thracians nor Athenians, but aliens of other stock (*Hell. Ath.*, pp. 219 ff.). Their earliest dated record (IG^2 II 1317b add.) belongs to the archonship of Hieron (254/3 B.C.), or, with Scheme B, to 245/4?, Lysitheides archon. There were, accordingly, at this time four societies (at least) in Attica organized for the worship of Bendis, three of *orgeones* — two in the Piraeus (one Thracian and the other Athenian) and one in the city (Thracian) — and one of *thiasotai* (other aliens) at Salamis.

Bendis in the Piraeus in the *pompe* from the civic hearth in the *prytaneum* to the shrine of Bendis in the harbor town (cf. *Priests of Asklepios*, p. 157; *Hell. Ath.*, p. 230). Of course Thracian *orgeones* of Bendis may have been organized in the "city" without a *hieron*, but hardly, doubtless, for long. The terms of their participation in the *pompe* were within the control of the parent society of Thracian *orgeones* in the Piraeus, and in Polystratos' archonship they were arranged, obviously for the first time. While other periods can, doubtless, be found suitable for a separatist movement on the part of the Thracians in Athens, and another year than 261/0 B.C. for the establishment of coöperation between the new and the old society, it cannot be denied that the period of the Chremonidean War, with its long rupture of relations between Piraeus and Athens, and the epoch immediately following the reunification of the two places through the capture of Athens by Antigonus, satisfy admirably the conditions disclosed by *IG*² II 1283. Wilhelm (*Oester. Jahresh.*, V, 1902, pp. 135 f.) assigns the document on the basis of the letter-forms to the "Jahrzehnte der ersten Hälfte und der Mitte" of the third century. Prior to 250 B.C. we have several vacancies. 289/8 or 282/1, 284/3, 280/79, 272/1, 267/6, and 265/4 B.C. are freely open, but the Chremonidean War excludes 267/6 and 265/4. The most likely alternative to 261/0 is 276/5. The Piraeus was separated from Athens between 289/8 and *ca.* 280/79 B.C. (*above*, p. 72). This excludes 284/3 and 282/1, in all probability; since, even if peace existed between Antigonus and Athens in these years (of which we cannot be sure), the organization of a *pompe* between the city and the harbor is extremely unlikely at a time when, as we may infer from IG^2 II 657 (285/4 B.C.), the Athenians were openly avowing their plans for regaining the Piraeus. Since the decree of the Thracians was passed on the eighth of Hekatombaion, 280/79 B.C. is perhaps too early. Moreover, this year belongs in all likelihood to Gorgias. It seems probable from what we have said above (pp. 72 f.) that the Piraeus was lost again by Athens in 275/4. This would make 276/5 B.C. an appropriate date for Polystratos; and, since the archon-name for 276/5 began with P, I have restored it as Polystratos. Apart from 261/0 B.C. there seems to be really no other place for Polystratos before 250 B.C.,[1] for in 272/1 B.C. the Piraeus and Athens were again separate. There are no other names beginning with P at our disposal and only six unknown archons to reckon with prior to 229/8 B.C.

It does not follow that Sosistratos belongs in 261/0 B.C., but the name suits the lacuna in IG^2 II 477 (*SEG*, III, 89), and the prosopographical evidence accords sufficiently (Dinsmoor, p. 187, n. 6). Yet for all this I should not suggest 261/0 for him except for the striking congruity of his name with those of the following archons. How did it come about that Athens had in a series an archon whose name meant "lover of the army," another whose name meant "exhibitor of the army," another whose name meant "sparer of the army," another whose name meant "capable of meeting in battle," and finally another whose name meant "renown in battle"? I cannot believe such a collocation of archon-

---

[1] Using Scheme B, Table II, several years following 256/5 B.C. are available.

names fortuitous. We have documentary proof that after 263/2 B.C. Antigonus took a hand in the appointment of Athenian generals and *hipparchs* (*SEG.*, III, 122),[1] and literary evidence (Hegesandros *ap. Athen.*, IV, 167e) that at least in one instance he appointed one of the Nine Archons. The latter instance shows that the king was not above indulging his humor at the expense of the Athenians. The text runs:

'Demetrius, the grandson of Demetrius of Phalerum,' as Hegesander says, 'went to such extremes of prodigality that he kept Aristagora of Corinth as his mistress and lived sumptuously. And when the Areopagites summoned him before them and bade him

---

[1] In this document the contrast between χειροτονηθείς and κατασταθείς (ἐπει[δὴ 'Απολλόδωρος κ]ατασταθείς στρατηγὸς ὑπό τε τοῦ βασιλέως 'Αντιγόνου, καὶ [ὑπὸ τοῦ δήμου] χειροτονηθείς ἐπὶ τὴν χώραν τὴν παραλίαν) is clear: the one means "elected" and the other "appointed." The same is the case in *SEG*, III, 123: [στρατηγὸς δὲ ἐπ'] 'Αντιμάχου ἄ[ρχοντος κατασταθείς ὑπὸ 'Αντιγόνου, ἵ]ππαρχός τε χε[ιροτονηθείς ὑπὸ τοῦ δήμου]. Κατασταθείς, in the sense of appointed, also occurs in *BCH*, 1930, p. 269, l. 5: Δικαίαρχος - - κατασταθείς μετὰ τοῦ πατρὸς 'Απολλωνίου ὑπὸ τοῦ βασιλέ[ως Δημητρίο]υ, and, doubtless, in line 15. But it is also used as a synonym for χειροτονηθείς. Thus in *IG* II² 1303 (220/19 B.C., archon Kallaischros), at a time when appointment of generals by the Macedonian king is excluded, we find [κατ]ασταθείς [δ]ὲ [σ]τρα[τηγὸς ἐ]πὶ τ[ὴ]ν [χ]ώραν [τὴν ἐπ' 'Ελευσ]ῖνο[ς] εἰς τ[ὸν ἐνιαυ]τὸν τὸν ἐπ[ὶ Κα]λλα[ίσχρου ἄρχοντος] in a context in which a contrast with χειροτονηθείς is almost implied (cf. ll. 5, 11). Again in *IG²* II 1281 (*ca.* 266 B.C.?) πρότερον κατασταθείς στ[ρατηγὸς ἐπὶ τοὺς] ὁπλίτας occurs, followed in line 6 by καὶ νῦν δὲ πάλιν χε[ιροτον]ηθείς στρατηγός; and in *IG²* II 1299, l. 59 κατασταθεί[ς τε στρατηγὸς ἐπ' 'Ελευ]σῖνος εἰς τὸν ἐπὶ Κίμωνος ἐνιαυτόν (237/6 B.C.), followed in line 64 by χειροτονηθείς τε τὸ δεύτερον στρατηγὸς ἐπ' 'Ελευσῖνος ε[ἰς τὸν ἐπὶ 'Εκφάντου ἐ]νιαυτόν (236/5 B.C.). Apart from desire to vary the expression, the use of κατασταθείς in the case of an officer designated by the *demos* was facilitated perhaps by the frequency with which generals, subsequent to election by *cheirotonia*, had to be "appointed" by some process or other to the specific posts in which they served. Τεταγμένος, used of Dikaiarchos in *BCH*, 1930, p. 269, l. 17, means "stationed."

live a better life, he replied, "But I am living as becomes a man of breeding as it is. For I have a mistress who is very fair, I have never wronged any man, I drink Chian wine, and in all other respects I contrive to satisfy myself, since my private revenues are sufficient for these purposes; I do not, as some of you do, live as a venal judge or adulterer." Thereupon he designated by name some who made a practice of these things. And when King Antigonus heard this, he made him a judge (θεσμοθέτην αὐτὸν κατέστησεν). At the Panathenaea as commander of horse (*hipparch*),[1] he reared beside the Hermae a platform for Aristagora higher than the Hermae; and at Eleusis, at the time of the Mysteries, he placed a throne for her beside the temple, after threatening that any one who should try to prevent him would be sorry for it.'[2]

It is possible that this sequence of oddly significant eponymous names is a piece of elaborate irony on the king's part; more likely, I think, that it was a demonstration, tantamount to an expression of confidence in their troops, on the part of the Athenians themselves. I take it as an interesting corroboration of my Tribal Cycles that they place this astonishing aggregate of archons between Arrheneides, who, it is to be noted, stands outside the aggregate, and the withdrawal of the Macedonian garrison from the city in 256/5 B.C.; and it is a notable coincidence that, if we accept Scheme A, Table II, they also assign to the year immediately following the recovery by Athens of its civic liberty an archon with the significant name "much-desired" (Polyeuktos).

The peculiarity of the archonship, was, of course, that its holder gave his name to the year. His name was

[1] A Demetrios (patronymic and demotic unknown) was appointed *hipparch* by Antigonus in 257/6 B.C. (*IG*² II 1285; *SEG*, III, 123; cf. Table I, above, p. 14). Though Demetrios is a very common name, it seems likely that he was the Phalerian.

[2] Translation by Gulick in the *Loeb Classics*.

blazoned on public and private documents and was carried with them to all parts of the world. It figured in correspondence (of the school-heads for example) and in business contracts. It was by his name that the periods were marked off in the local *Atthides*, and in other chronicles, histories, and chronological tables. It was used by astronomers and makers of calendars (*parapegmata*) at home and abroad. Its vogue was so considerable that it was employed either alone (*IG*^{2} II 1135) or in conjunction with local *eponymi* or other indications of time in far distant cities (Lyttos, Magnesia, Delphi). We are not surprised, accordingly, that the Athenians gave the office (sortition was circumvented somehow [1]) to men whose names conveyed a message which contemporaries were probably better able to understand than we are. There is not much ambiguity in the name Hierophantes attached to 86/5 B.C.: Athens was proclaimed thereby as the city of the Eleusinian Mysteries, and as such entitled to veneration (which Sulla himself recognized by becoming an initiate), despite the "misdeeds" of philosophers and democrats, the burning of the Odeum, and the reduction of the Piraeus to a heap of ruins. But what did the Athenians mean when in 166/5 B.C. they gave the archonship to Achaios and in 165/4 to Pelops? The choice of two men of such names to hold the eponymous office in these years cannot lack significance. The Achaeans, it will be recalled, received the Delians in 166 B.C., when they were required to evacuate the island to make room for the Athenian cleruchs, gave them their citizenship, and

[1] It is conceivable, for example, that none of the *phyletae* other than the individual with the desired name participated in the allotment.

championed their financial claims against Athens even to the extent of authorizing reprisals (ῥύσια) and carrying their case to Rome (*Polyb.*, XXXII, 7; *Hell. Ath.*, pp. 323 f.; *CAH*, VIII, p. 294). Are we to assume that Athens was at first grateful to the Achaeans for taking the Delians off their hands and treating them thus generously, and that the quarrel which was carried to Rome in *ca.* 159–8 B.C. (Büttner-Wobst) [1] was an unexpected aftermath? Or is the choice first of Achaios and then of Pelops a mere pleasantry? However that may be, we see that the Hellenistic Athenians *did* embody in their archon-names allusions to contemporary situations and events.

The specific reason assigned in IG^2 II 791 (Diomedon archon, 253/2 B.C.) for the solicitation of subscriptions "for the safety of the state and the protection of the countryside" was to provide the treasurer of the military fund, Eurykleides of Kephisia, with the money needed "to harvest in security the crops during the remainder of the year." The time of the launching of the project was the last day of Elaphebolion (April 8th, 252 B.C., Dinsmoor). That an emergency levy had thus to be made in this spring is intelligible. As nearly as can be ascertained, this was the very time of the secession of Alexander, Krateros' son (Beloch, *Griech. Gesch.*, IV 2, pp. 518 ff.; Tarn, *CAH*, VII, pp. 221 ff.; Dinsmoor, pp. 110, 180), and the opening of the war between him and Antigonus in which Attica was attacked from two sides, from Corinth and Eretria. At this moment Herakleitos of Athmonon commanded the Macedonian

[1] I am unable to control this date. Niese (*Gesch. d. griech. u. maked. Staaten*, III, p. 191, n. 6; cf. p. 4, n. 1) suggests "etwa 157 v. Chr."

forces in the Piraeic district (IG^2 II 1225, 677).[1] Athens ultimately bought off the assailants with Argive assistance (IG^2 II 774; *SEG*, III, 98, 249/8 B.C.). It cannot be denied that the dating of Diomedon in 253/2 B.C. accords well with the demands of historical facts.

Should, however, line four of IG^2 II 791 be restored with a secretary from Leukonoe (*above*, pp. 18 f.), and Diomedon be regarded as a second archon of that name, the resultant date, 232/1 B.C., likewise permits a plausible adjustment between the contents of the decree and the historical situation (*Hell. Ath.*, pp. 203 ff.). It yields an equally satisfactory construction of the *cursus honorum* of Eurykleides of Kephisia (archon, 249/8; *tamias*, 232/1; *prostates* τοῦ δήμου, 229–211; *akme*, ca. 245 B.C.), and it brings the activity of [Diogen]es Make(don) in subscribing for the defense of Attica (Wilhelm, IG^2 II 791 add., note) into closer juxtaposition with his extraordinary manifestation of phil-Athenianism in 229 B.C.

I should like to emphasize again (cf. *Priests of Asklepios*, pp. 155 f.) the appositeness of a scheme of

[1] After 263/2 B.C. Attica was divided into three military districts, the Piraeic, the Eleusinian, and the Paralian (see *above*, Table I, and *Klio*, 1909, pp. 316 ff.). Antigonus retained the appointment of the general of the first in his own hands, and kept him in office for years on end. To the other two districts he appointed members of the annually changing board of Athenian generals. The troops were in part Athenian citizens, in part ξένοι, the latter, like the former (IG^2 II 1300), commanded by subordinate (usually foreign) *hegemones*, or captains (IG^2 II 1286, 1299, 1310). We do not know whether Diogenes received the Athenian citizenship (Wilhelm, *Beiträge z. griech. Inschriftenkunde*, Sonderschr. d. Oester. Arch. Inst., VII, p. 81; *Hell. Ath.*, pp. 201, 425) before or after his appointment to the Piraeic command. In 252 B.C. he was still a Macedonian. Demetrius retained his father's system (*BCH*, 1930, pp. 269 f.). After 229 B.C. the ξένοι and *hegemones* remained (IG^2 II 1300, 1312).

cycles which dates Thersilochos in 244/3 B.C.: no better time could be imagined than the year following the battle of Chaeronea (245 B.C.) for the arbitration of disputes between the Boeotians and the Athenians (IG^2 II 778, 779) and the designation of Lamia as arbitrator.

There is no doubt that Dinsmoor's cycle (p. 179) places Athenodoros (restoring this name in IG^2 II 798, l. 10) in an appropriate year (243/2 B.C.); but 240/39 B.C. is equally appropriate. The Aetolians were allies of Macedon from 243/2 to 238/7 B.C., and in 241 B.C. they made their notorious attack on the Achaeans, Antigonus' enemy. Aratus made a raid into Attica and attempted to surprise the Piraeus in the spring of 240 B.C. (Tarn, *CAH*, VII, p. 735); hence the grant by the *agonothetes* of special honors to the Aetolians at the Dionysia of 240 B.C., and the collection of subscriptions by Athens "for the protection of the countryside" in the course of the year,[1] are apposite.

It has been pointed out already (*above*, p. 13) that (barring grave irregularities) Apollonios cannot have been appointed general by Demetrius (*BCH*, 1930, pp. 268 ff.; IG^2 II 1299) in 242/1 or 241/0 B.C., as required by Dinsmoor's cycles. By mine he received the appointment in 239/8, than which nothing could be happier.

---

[1] Should we accept Scheme B, Table II, these subscriptions would cover the second half of 240 B.C., those of IG^2 II 791 its first half. The *cursus honorum* of Eurykleides would be, *tamias* in 241/0, archon in 232/1, and *prostates* in 230/29 ff.

VIII. Tribal Cycles, Archons, and Priests between 230/29 and 201/0 b.c.

It cannot, I think, be denied that there is a singular felicity in a system which dates in 230/29 b.c. the opening of the famous list of *archontes*, *IG*² II 1706 (see *above*, Table III, p. 50). A new epoch began for Athens with its recovery in that year of its independence.[1] The date is certain (Dinsmoor, p. 509). The list ended with Herakleitos (213/2; 209/8 b.c., Dinsmoor) — on my scheme, as on Dinsmoor's, with the close of a secretary-cycle. We have, accordingly, another instance (see *above*, pp. 43 f., 61) in which the Athenians recognized Tribal Cycles in the making of public records. Further cases of this practice have been pointed out by Dinsmoor: 343/2 b.c. is the end of the first part and 342/1 the beginning of the second part of the inventory of the Asklepieion formed by joining *IG*² II 1532 with 1533 (Dinsmoor, pp. 453 f.), and 342/1 b.c. had a priest from Erechtheis (I); the "great list" of eponymous archons (*IG*² II 1713; Ditt., *Syll.*³, 733) began in 145/4 b.c. (Dinsmoor, pp. 234, 282 ff.), again with a new secretary-cycle, the first to follow the momentous events of 146 b.c. We note, further, that 279/8 b.c. (again the first year of the secretary-cycle) was the year in which the building was erected on which were inscribed the earlier records (*didaskaliae*) of the tragedies and comedies performed at the Dionysia and

---

[1] It is to be noted (*si licet parva comparare magnis*) that the catalogue of *epimeletae* of a Salaminian *thiasos* (*SEG*, II, 9) began with those of Polyeuktos' archonship. According to Scheme A, Table II, this was the first year (255/4 b.c.) of Athenian civic liberty.

Lenaea (IG^2 II 2319–2323) together with the earlier *catalogi victorum* at the same fêtes (IG^2 II 2325), both sets of lists being continued thereafter by different hands at different times. The original compilation was thus terminated with the close of a Tribal Cycle (Dinsmoor, pp. 464 ff.).[1] The great list of priests of Sarapis, which probably began in 145/4 B.C. with a priest from Erechtheis (Dinsmoor, p. 234), ended with the completion of a Tribal Cycle in 110/9 B.C.; a new list of the priests of Asklepios began with Erechtheis (I) in 109/8 B.C. (IG^2 II 1944). Obviously the limits of Tribal Cycles served as punctuation points in the publication (*anagraphe*) of records in Athens. This is intelligible when we reflect that they marked off the administrative periods for so many of the routine services (see *above*, p. 49).

The formulae of dating used in IG^2 II 838 (a decree of the archonship of Ergochares) can be interpreted and restored most satisfactorily, Dinsmoor urges (pp. 193 ff.), on the assumption that the year was an intercalary year of the epoch of the thirteen tribes. The point is arguable (p. 194, n. 3). His further contention that "the twelve tribes alone were in existence as late as the appointment of the secretary for the year" of Ergochares is probably correct, but it is not established, as alleged, by the fact that *he* came from Antiochis, his predecessor from Aiantis: it would be established only if his deme, Alopeke, were one of the demes transferred to Ptolemais, which is not the case, or if a rupture of the secretary-cycle inevitably accompanied the creation

---

[1] It seems to me probable that the addenda began with 279/8, instead of 278/7 B.C. as assumed by Dinsmoor (p. 464).

pographia of Athens for this time shows, it was in 263 B.C., and not in 229, that the radical change in the personnel of the governing society in Attica occurred. It was not till the surrender of the Achaean League to Antigonus in the spring of 224 B.C., when Athens found itself menaced by the encircling power of its traditional enemies, that Eurykleides and Mikion awoke to the necessity of cultivating the friendship of Ptolemy, who had meanwhile commended himself to them as the most likely protector of the neutrality of Athens by various marks of consideration (*IG*² II 838; cf. 1303) and by the support he was giving to Kleomenes of Sparta (Plut., *Agis*, 22, 3; Tarn, *CAH*, VII, pp. 758 ff.; *Hell. Ath.*, pp. 240 ff.). Furthermore, to date Ergochares in 229/8 B.C. means to reject the archon-cycles established above (Table III, pp. 50 ff.): the year 230/29 B.C., when a cycle would begin, would precede the recovery by Athens of its independence; and the beginning of earlier cycles would be 242/1, 254/3, and 266/5 B.C. We should not find a significant date for the inauguration of archon-cycles even if we went back to the fourth century; whereas, on dating Ergochares in 226/5 B.C., the archon-cycles are inaugurated in precisely the right year (263/2 B.C.). A further and, as it seems to me, fatal consequence of dating Ergochares in 229/8 B.C. is that Heliodoros is thereby placed in 232/1. It then follows that already in 232/1 B.C. the Athenians had recast their institutions into the form in which they meet us thereafter (*IG*² II 844A).[1] That this should have been

[1] The characteristic feature of the democratic-nationalist regime is the transfer of the administration of finance (ἐπὶ τῇ διοικήσει) from an individual to a commission. The commission was created in 288 B.C. (Dinsmoor, p.

done at least three years before they regained their freedom is an anachronism. It constituted one of the initial improbabilities which led me from the start to reserve judgment regarding the correctness of Dinsmoor's Tribal Cycles for this whole period. And, finally, the attribution of Ergochares, with a secretary from Antiochis, to 226/5 and of Thrasyphon, with a secretary from Pandionis, to 221/0 B.C. is now pivoted on the dating of *Inschr. von Magnesia*, no. 37, with a secretary from Aigeis, in 209/8 B.C. (*above*, p. 36, n. 8; *below*, pp. 128 f., notes). There cannot, I think, be the slightest doubt that the current Tribal Cycles between 230/29 and 201/0 B.C. are correct.

There was nothing in the creation of the new *phyle* to require the disruption of the priestly and secretary cycles: demes were simply taken from all the ten old *phylae*, and a new deme (Berenikidai) created, to constitute the new tribal aggregate, Ptolemais, which furnished the priest of Asklepios in 220/19 and the secretary in 219/8 B.C. when its regular turn came. It is conceivable that, as a further honor to Ptolemy, Ptolemais should have been given the first place in

12), when Athens gained its independence, and superseded by an individual in 263/2 B.C., when it lost it. The delegation of the office to one man facilitated royal control of this important function of government. That it should have ended while Athens remained a Macedonian dependency would be quite out of accord with the earlier history of this function. After 229 B.C. either the commission or the treasurer of military funds alone, or the two jointly are entrusted with the task of paying for the *anagraphe* of public decrees. This is a new rôle for the treasurer. His appearance, apparently in a similar capacity (the significant phrase is a restoration), in 276/5 B.C. (IG^2 II 1534A, l. 15) is an isolated occurrence, attributable, perhaps, to the extraordinary size and expense of the *stele* required for the inventory of the Asklepieion.

a new cycle of secretaries; but, as the tribal relations of the secretaries in 226-4 and 221/0 B.C. (Thrasyphon) show, this was not done. As pointed out above (p. 53), the archon-cycle needed and got readjustment.

On the assumption that the list of *archontes* IG^2 II 1706 began with the board which held office in the year Athens regained its liberty, 230/29 B.C., — the most probable assumption surely,[1] — one year, and one year only, is possible for Diokles, namely 215/4 B.C. A glance at Table IV, in which the disposition of the names on the stone[2] is exhibited (the eponymous archon doing service for himself and his colleagues) will establish this fact.

Since Diokles belonged to the epoch of the thirteen *phylae* (IG^2 II 847), the only other place for him is 202/1 B.C. Should we accept this alternative, for which nothing favorable can be said, we should have to assume that after Thrasyphon col. I contained fourteen lists of *archontes*; whereupon col. I would have had 241 lines and col. II only 50 — an unlikely conclusion. And there is in fact a fatal objection to the later possibility. 202/1 B.C. is the third year of the Olympiad, whereas in Diokles' year the Great Eleusinia were celebrated,

---

[1] Conversely, with Thrasyphon, col. i, in 221/0 B.C. and Diokles, col. ii, in 215/4 B.C. the earliest possible year for the first list in col. i is 233/2 B.C., the latest 230/29 B.C. On Dinsmoor's dates (Thrasyphon, col. i in 221/0 B.C. and Diokles, col. ii, 211/0 B.C.) the upper and lower limits for the first list in col. i are 240/39 and 233/2 B.C. He makes the catalogue begin with the upper limit because 240/39 B.C. is, on his dating, the first year after the accession of Demetrius to the throne of Macedon.

[2] The stone was prepared to a width sufficient to accommodate two further columns of names (each covering a Tribal Cycle of 13 years); but with an inconsequence of which Attic documents furnish other examples these were never added.

CYCLES, ARCHONS, AND PRIESTS, 230/201 B.C.   97

which came in the second year of the Olympiad, as Dinsmoor (pp. 209 ff.) has proved beyond any possibility of doubt. Hence on the premises Diokles belonged in 215/4 B.C. (Ol. 141, 2), whereupon we establish the happy "coincidence" that the scrutiny of the votives in the Asklepieion made in his year occurred at the end of the priestly cycle (IG^2 II 1539; cf. *above*,

TABLE IV

Year	Archon	Year	Archon
	Col. I		Col. II
230/9	——	217/6	——
229/8	Heliodoros	216/5	-s
228/7	Leochares <————>	215/4	Diokles
227/6	Theophilos	214/3	Euphiletos
226/5	Ergochares	213/2	Herakleitos
225/4	Niketes		
224/3	Antiphilos		*Vacat*
223/2	(gap)		
222/1	Menekrates		
221/0	Thrasyphon		
220/9	——		
219/8	——		
218/7	——		

p. 44). The alternate date for Diokles, the one demanded by Dinsmoor's system (211/0 B.C.), fails to satisfy this desideratum. That the Great Eleusinia were in fact celebrated in Diokles' year is stated in IG^2 II 1304, ll. 24 ff.: "and seeing that the fête of the Great Eleusinia fell in the years in which he was general, Demainetos sacrificed to the Two Divinities, *etc.*" Demainetos was general in the archonships of Chairephon, Diokles, and Aischron. It was straining the natural meaning of the Greek when I suggested (*Athenian Archons*, p. 42) that it would suffice for the Great Eleusinia to have been celebrated in two of the three years which came in question, and when A. Mommsen, Dittenberger, and Kirchner (*GGA*, 1900, p. 449) thought that one celebration alone was involved. Kolbe (*Die attischen Archonten*, Abh. Gesell. Wiss. Goett., N. F., X, 4, pp. 68 ff.) very properly pointed this out, and both Kirchner (*IG*^{2} II iv, p. 16) and I (*Hell. Ath.*, p. 248, n. 2) have tacitly let our interpretation drop. Even though my suggestion were acceptable, we should have now to hold that the two years were those of Chairephon and Diokles; for among the recent finds in the agora of Athens is an inscription (as yet unpublished) which shows that the secretary of Chairephon's year came from the deme Kydantidai (Ptolemais, VII), i.e., according to the Tribal Cycle four years before Diokles. We have herein a notable confirmation of the existence in this epoch of the Tribal Cycles, but no further aid in determining what this Tribal Cycle was, since in Dinsmoor's system Chairephon and Diokles also fall in the second years of Olympiads, Chairephon in 215/4 and Diokles in 211/0 B.C. Apart from the arguments presented to establish the validity of one system and the invalidity of the other (which seem to me conclusive), we are still limited on this point to the information contained in the introductory part of *IG*^{2} II 1304, where prior to the mention of his generalship in Chairephon's archonship it is said of Demainetos that "he went several times as ambassador to the Aetolian League and also to Philip to the end that their friendship and peace with Athens might be preserved, and that, drawn into the struggle by neither, the state might be restored to its pristine prosperity. In this connection he shrank from no hardship or danger, but furthered the interests of his country both by word and act. In return Athens commended him repeatedly and crowned him with a gold crown, thus repaying the benefits it had received with meet rewards." The reference to negotiations conducted at the outbreak of the Social War (220 B.C.) is clear and unequivocal, but these could have been mentioned appropriately by way of introduction to services rendered during a generalship whether this was held in 219/8 or 215/4 B.C., with a certain preponderance of appropriateness, perhaps, in favor of the earlier year. It would, however, be surprising if Athens withheld the generalship from so deserving a man as Demainetos till two years after the war was over.

Using the methods employed by Dinsmoor (p. 164) we can determine that the only years open to an archon Euandros and a priest of Asklepios from Aigeis or Kekropis, Timokles of Halai (Sundwall, *Nachträge z. Prosopographia Attica*, p. 160; Kirchner, IG^2 II iv, p. 17, n*), between 277/6 and 200 B.C. are 242/1, 230/29, 217/6, and 204/3. Using letter-forms as his criterion Kirchner dates the dedication, in which Timokles appears, in the middle of the third century. In view of the chaos which reigns at present in the history of letter-forms during this entire period, Dinsmoor (pp. 214 ff., 509) seeks another way of determining the epoch of Euandros and Timokles. On grounds which seem to me valid he has brought together IG^2 II 845 and 652; and since 652 as well as 845 belongs after 229

B.C.,[1] he identifies quite properly the Diokles who appears as archon in line seven of 652 with the Diokles whom we have placed in 215/4 B.C. He proceeds further and tentatively joins the two stones in such a way that 652 becomes the conclusion of the decree of which the beginning is preserved in 845, ll. 23 ff. It thus appears that an archon . . . . . rou (in the genitive) was in office some time after 215/4 B.C. The identification of . . . . . ros with Euandros is very attractive (we lack only five archon-names between 277/6 and 213/2 and none of those we possess fits the space except Euandros); but the argument by which . . . . . ros is dated after 215/4 is not cogent. An examination of the stones made for me by Mr. Sterling Dow shows decisively that IG^2 II 845, ll. 23 ff. is not to be joined with IG^2 II 652: the *stelae* differ in thickness, treatment of the surface and margin, spacing and direction of the lines, spacing of the letters, and width of margins. "Everything seems to oppose their being joined." All that we are warranted in saying is that IG^2 II 652 and 845 deal with the same persons (Aischron, son of Proxenos, of Delphi, and his associates). IG^2 II 845A, in which they are praised by Athens and given the prospect of Athenian citizenship if they desire it is obviously earlier than IG^2 II 652 in which Aischron receives the citizenship. IG^2 II 652 was passed shortly after the archonship of Diokles (215/4 B.C.). In IG^2 II 845A the services for which Aischron

[1] Kirchner, note on IG^2 II 845. The appearance of the title γραμματεὺς τῆς β[ουλῆς καὶ τοῦ δήμου] or γραμματεὺς τῆς β[ουλῆς] in line 34 of IG^2 II 652 is unique, the first at any period, the last after 318/7 B.C. (*Athenian Secretaries*, p. 64; Brillant, *Les secrétaires athéniens*, p. 120, n. 2). Between 229 and 200 B.C. the publication-formulas of decrees were less stereotyped than before or after (Dinsmoor, pp. 203 f.).

was honored were enumerated. The beginning of the decree is lost. As we have it, it opens with a reference to a gift of grain and ends with some favors done to "envoys from Athens." It seems likely therefore, that the service rendered in Diokles' year — the liberation from slavery of Athenian captives — was performed subsequent to the time of IG^2 II 845A; and, since this service was the occasion for the grant of Athenian citizenship, such was indubitably the case. IG^2 II 845A contains a passage beginning "on peace being made, if any of them decide to be enrolled as citizens of Athens" (εἰρήνης δὲ γενομένη[s ἐάν τινες αὐτῶν γράψασθαι π]ολιτῶν βουλεύωνται Ἀθη[ναίων]). Since the document precedes 215/4 B.C. the reference must be to the Peace of Naupaktos which ended the Social War, and the date must be in or shortly before the autumn of 217 B.C. We do not know the contents of IG^2 II 845B, which gives us the name of the archon . . . . . ros; but since it is inscribed, apparently by the same hand, on the same stone, it probably contained a vote of commendation for one of the associates of Aischron mentioned in IG^2 II 845A along with him as "benefactors" of Athens. We should consequently date IG^2 II 845B in or about 217/6 B.C.

A restoration of the secretary's name in IG^2 II 845B, already made by Kirchner, enables us to arrive at a precise date. Unfortunately the stone lacks the part essential for our purpose, the *demotikon*; and we cannot ascertain the number of letter-spaces this occupied. On the basis of IG^2 II 448, l. 36 (Θέρσιππος Ἱππο[θέρσους Ἀχαρνε]ύς; cf. *PA*, 7615, 8068) and IG^1 II 1939 (Σωσικλῆς Θρασίππου Ἀχαρνεύς; cf. *PA*, 13234) Kirchner has restored the reading of the stone, . ερσ . . . . . . ρασ - - -, as [Θ]έρσ[ιππος Θ]ρασ[ίππου 'Αχαρνεύς]. Of course a chain is no stronger than its weakest link; but seeing that a secretary from Acharnai (Oineis IX) in the archonship of . . . . . ros and the priest from Halai (Kekropis X or Aigeis IV) in the archonship of Euandros combine to date IG^2 II 845B in the year (217/6 B.C.) to which we have been led by historical considerations, the weakest link is materially strengthened. It then follows that IG^2 II 783, a decree of the epoch of the thirteen tribes, with a secretary from Epikephisia (Oineis IX), belongs in 204/3 B.C. or later. A decree from the agora of Athens (as yet unpublished) with the same secretary will probably give us the archon-name.

IX. THE EPHEBE LISTS OF THE THIRD CENTURY B.C.

IT HAS long been noticed (*Priests of Asklepios*, pp. 162 ff.) that subsequent to the abolition of national conscription of ephebes (*post* 305/4 B.C., IG^2 II 478, rather *post* 303/2 B.C., IG^2 II 1159; *ante* 269/8, IG^2 II 665) the practice of drawing up the annual lists under both tribal and deme captions was maintained, though the subdivision of the lads into deme groups to the number of 175 was not called for once the ephebes had become fewer than 30. The earlier practice was followed in 269/8 B.C. (IG^2 II 665): the later practice of using the tribal captions alone is found in the lists for the years of Polyeuktos (IG^2 II 681, 255/4 B.C.), Philoneos (IG^2 II 766), and Kimon (IG^2 II 787, 237/6 B.C.) as well as in the lists of the second century (IG^2 II 1006, 1008, 1009, 1011, 1028) and later (IG^2 II 1039, 1043). The change of practice is best accounted for by the events of 263/2 B.C. We have no evidence that an ephebe corps existed between 263/2 and 256/5 B.C.; but we have no evidence that it did not exist, since the argument from silence — the absence of ephebe documents during this period — is valueless. Equally long gaps are frequently found in our corpus of ephebe records. Consequently all we can affirm with assurance regarding the archonship of Philoneos is that it falls after 268/7 B.C.[1] It probably belongs after 263/2 and possibly after 256/5 B.C.

We have also an ephebe record, from which, however, the catalogue of ephebes is lost, for the year preceding the archonship of Thymochares (IG^2 II 700). The name of the archon is lost, but it had ten (or nine) letters in the genitive, and the year was probably intercalary (Dinsmoor, p. 395). This archon, and consequently Thymochares, belongs before Philoneos. This conclusion rests upon an examination of the lists of officials of the ephebe corps. They are presented in Table V.

In the year preceding that of Thymochares we have either one of two things: (1) the *kosmetes* was listed exceptionally along with the other *didaskaloi* (he is ordinarily isolated as the recipient of special honors),

[1] A comparatively late date is indicated for Philoneos by certain prosopographical evidence. Ainesidemos of Sypalettos, ephebe in his year, became king-archon under Menekrates (222/1 B.C.), and Eunikos of Sphettos, also an ephebe in his year, became *thesmothetes* under Herakleitos (213/2 B.C.). If Philoneos belongs in 242/1 B.C., the one was 38, the other 47 when he became a member of the board of Nine Archons. Naturally they may have been each 20 years older on attaining this dignity. Should we place Philoneos in 261/0 B.C. in place of Sosistratos, we should have to date Thymochares in 265/4 or 267/6 B.C. But is it likely that the son of Phaidros of Sphettos was archon at the time of the Chremonidean War?

TABLE V

I. Meneklés, 269/8 b.c.
(IG^2 II 665)

	Kosmetes	Ameinias, son of Antiphanes, of Kephisia
1	Paidotribes	Hermodoros, son of Heortios, of Acharnai
3	Akontistes	Philotheos, son of Stratios, of Lamptrai
5	Katapaltaphetes	Mnesitheos, son of Mnesitheos, of Kopros
	Grammateus	Hermogenes
4	Toxotes	Sondron of Crete

II. Polyeuktos, 255/4 b.c.
(IG^2 II 681)

	Kosmetes	—— —— of Rhamnus
1	Paidotribes	Hermodoros, son of Heortios, of Acharnai

III. Year before Thymochares
(IG^2 II 700)

	——	-onides, son of Androkles, of ——
1	Paidotribes	Hermodoros, son of Heortios, of Acharnai
3	Akontistes	Lysikles, son of Antipatros, of Sypalettos
	——	——, son of Nikandros, of Ankyle
4	Toxotes	—— —— ——
	Grammateus	—— —— ——

IV. Philoneos
(IG^2 II 766)

	Kosmetes	——, son of -kles, of Euonymon
1	Paidotribes	Hermodoros, son of Heortios, of Acharnai
3	Akontistes	Lysikles, son of Antipatros, of Sypalettos
2	Hoplomachos	Charisandros, son of ——, of Halimus
4	Toxotes	Aristodemos
	Grammateus	——

V. Kimon, 237/6 b.c.
(IG^2 II 787)
All names of officials lost

VI. Unpublished Inscription

	Kosmetes	—— —— ——
1	Paidotribes	Heortios, son of Hermodoros, of Acharnai

3	Akontistes	Lysikles, son of Antipatros, of Sypalettos
2	Hoplomachos	Charisandros, son of ——, of Halimus
4	Toxotes	Aristokrates of Crete
5	Katapaltaphetes	Pedieus, son of ——, of Oe
	Grammateus	Herakleides, son of ——, of Kephisia

VII. IG^2 II 944b Add.
(After creation of Ptolemais)

	Kosmetes	—— —— ——
1	Paidotribes	Heortios, son of Hermodoros, of Acharnai
3	Akontistes	—— —— ——
2	Hoplomachos	—— —— ——
5	Katapaltaphetes	-dron, son of Pedieus, of Kerameikos
4	Toxotes	—— —— ——
	Grammateus	—— —— ——

VIII. Eupolemos, 185/4 b.c.
(IG^2 II 900)

	Kosmetes	Theobulos, son of O-, of ——
2	Hoplomachos	Persaios, son of Symmachos, of Kikynna
1	Paidotribes	Hermodoros, son of Heortios, of Acharnai
3	Akontistes	-n, son of Nikomachos, of Aphidna
5	Katapaltaphetes	—— —— ——
	Grammateus	Soson, son of Proxenos, of Sphettos

A. In the later documents (123/2–102/1 b.c.) the order of the officials is invariably 1, 2, 3, 4, 5.

in which case -onides, son of Androkles, was *kosmetes*; or (2) there were six officials in addition to the *kosmetes*, as in the new inscription from the agora. In the first case —, son of Nikandros, of Ankyle was *hoplomachos* (the *katapaltaphetes* being absent, as in Philoneos' year); in the second the two officials -onides, son of Androkles, and —, son of Nikandros, of Ankyle were *hoplomachos* and *katapaltaphetes*. In any case Charisandros of Halimus was not *hoplomachos*. Since he was *hoplomachos* both in Philoneos' year and in that of the new document, the chances are (assuming continuity in tenure of this office) that Thymochares and his predecessor came earlier than Philoneos. The earliest date (apart from 261/0 B.C., for which see *above*, pp. 77, n. 1, 81 ff.) which fulfils the conditions already stated for Thymochares — a predecessor with ten (or nine) letters in the genitive of his name; an intercalary year — is 243/2 B.C. Philoneos can then be assigned to 242/1 or 241/0 B.C.[1]

Since the new inscription from the agora lacks the name of the archon any desired year is open for it. It clearly belongs later than Philoneos: in Philoneos' year Hermodoros of Acharnai was *paidotribes*; in the new year his son Heortios held this office. Heortios was himself an ephebe in Philoneos' year. Conceivably he was qualified for appointment as *paidotribes* once his ephebate was completed; but we should preferably date his appointment a few years later. It may have been accelerated by the possible death or incapacity of his father who had held the office for at least 28 years (assuming 242/1 B.C. for Philoneos). An early date for the new inscription is indicated by the fact that Lysikles of Sypalettos was *akontistes*. We have dated his priesthood of Asklepios in 266/5 B.C. If he were 30 + years of age when he became priest he would have been a man of 55 + in Philoneos' year. Presumably an *akontistes* had to be a person of some physical activity. The new inscription may, therefore, be dated in the epoch 241/0–235/4 B.C.

As the list of ephebe officials shows (Table V), the new

---

[1] If we accept Scheme B, Table II, no precise years can be assigned to Thymochares and Philoneos.

inscription reveals a change in the composition of the staff of ephebe officials. In Philoneos' year there were only five *didaskaloi*: in the new record there are six. The new office is the *katapaltaphetes*. There was a *katapaltaphetes* in 269/8 B.C. There was possibly none in the year preceding Thymochares (244/3? B.C.). There was certainly none in Philoneos' year. A change of this sort can have occurred at any time. It is intelligible that an expert trainer of the ephebes in handling katapults was felt to be desirable because of Aratus' attempt on the Piraeus in the spring of 240 B.C. or because of the incidents of the Demetrieian War (238/7 ff. B.C.); but his presence or absence may have no particular significance: there was no *hoplomachos* in 269/8 B.C.

Heortios was still *paidotribes* at the time of IG^2 II 944b add. That is to say, he was still serving after 224/3 B.C. His son, Hermodoros, was in turn *paidotribes* in 185/4 B.C. Grandfather, son, and grandson covered a span of at least 85 years — from 269/8 to 185/4 B.C. They must in each case have assumed the charge early in life. The son (Hermodoros 2d) of a man (Heortios) who was an ephebe in 242/1 B.C. may have been himself an ephebe in *ca.* 218 B.C. and become *paidotribes* a few years later.

X. The Archon Polyeuktos and the Aetolian Soteria

The concurrence of the secretary-cycle and the priestly cycle of Asklepios in dating Diomedon in 253/2 B.C. involves necessarily the dating of Polyeuktos in 255/4 B.C.; for the "closed" sequence, Polyeuktos, Hieron, Diomedon, is documentarily established (*SEG*, II, 9). In

Polyeuktos' year, on the thirtieth of the ninth prytany and the twenty-ninth of Elaphebolion (April 1st, Dinsmoor), Athens accepted the invitation of the Aetolians and their general Charixenos to participate in the Soteria, a festival which they had decided to establish in honor of Zeus Soter and Apollo Pythios in commemoration of the defeat of the Gauls in 279 B.C. (IG^2 II 680). Since the Aetolian Soteria fell between midsummer and the autumnal equinox (Beloch, *Griech. Gesch.*, IV 2, p. 492), the earliest date at which the first celebration of this festival can have occurred is the archonship of Hieron (Ol. 131, 3). Since, moreover, the dispatch of the invitation in March of 254 presupposes a celebration in the August–September next following, we may affirm, on the basis of the data thus far considered, that the first Aetolian Soteria were celebrated in the archonship of Hieron in Ol. 131, 3. But the Pythia were also celebrated in the third years of the Olympiad, in Metageitnion (August–September). Hence the Pythia and the Aetolian Soteria must have formed virtually one continuous festival, the Pythia honoring Apollo, the Soteria, Apollo and Zeus Soter; and, indeed, the coincidence of the two is suggested by the conjunction of their names with a single article in the frequently recurring phrase τὰ Πύθια καὶ Σωτήρια.[1]

[1] For festivals thus coupled see Segre, "Note epigrafiche," *Il Mondo Classico*, II, 1932, pp. 288 ff. The article combines the Nemea and Heraia at Argos (*Mnemosyne*, 1916, p. 65, ll. 16 ff.), its repetition separates the Dionysia and the Seleukeia at Erythrae (Ditt., *Syll.*³, 412/3). The use of a single article with the Dionysia and Demetreia in Euboea (*IG* XII 9, 207) is also associative, though the fêtes were not synchronous. If Dinsmoor, p. 8, l. 42, means, as Segre maintains, that in Athens Dionysia and Demetrieia came in alternate years, we should expect ἀγῶσι instead of ἀγῶνι (*IG*² II 891, 956, *et passim*); cf. Nock, *Harvard Studies*, 1930, pp. 60 f.

That the Aetolian Soteria were penteteric results from the most obvious restoration and interpretation of the much controverted passage of the Chian vote of acceptance of the new fête (Ditt., *Syll.*³, 402): "three *theori* shall be elected from all the Chians when this decree is ratified; for the future the designation of *theori* shall take place every four years at the time when *theori* [for the Pythia] are appointed" (ἐλέσθ[αι δὲ τὸ μὲν αὐτίκα θεω]ροὺς τρεῖς ἐκ πάντων Χίων, ὅταν τόδε τὸ ψήφισμα χειροτονηθῇ· γενέσ[θαι δὲ εἰς τὸ λοιπὸν] τὴν ἀπόδειξιν τῶν θεωρῶν καθ' ἑκάστην πενταετηρίδα, ὅταν καὶ [οἱ εἰς τὰ Πύθια [1] καθιστ]ῶνται).

Delphi has now yielded records for eleven distinct celebrations of the Aetolian Soteria. Flacelière (*BCH*, 1928, p. 281) arranges them in chronological order, the first in 254 B.C., the last in 214 B.C. Dinsmoor does likewise (p. 122), placing the first in 248 B.C., the last in 208 B.C. It must be conceded that, while there are certain limiting factors (notably the attested occurrences of Pythia, and the number of the Aetolian *hieromnemones*, which rose with the growth of their League and fell with its dismemberment), the Delphian records, taken by themselves, seem to permit a chronological divergence of this extent. In the present state of our knowledge the dating of the records of the Soteria, and hence of the Delphian archons of the third century, depends upon the year to be assigned to the Attic archon Polyeuktos.

The Delphian records of the Soteria seem to me to be irreconcilable with a date later than 251/0 B.C. for

[1] Alternate restorations: οἱ λοιποὶ θεωροί (De Sanctis, *Riv. di Fil.*, 1929, p. 572); εἰς τὰ 'Ολύμπια αἱρέ]ωνται (Pomtow, Ditt., *Syll.*³, 402; Beloch, *Griech. Gesch.*, IV 2, p. 493).

Polyeuktos when we hold fast to the two issues thus far reached in the discussion of the chronology of Delphi during this period (Dinsmoor, pp. 112 ff.; Flacelière, *BCH*, 1929, p. 431): (1) that the number of the Aetolian *hieromnemones* increased steadily with the territorial annexations made by the League and decreased with its losses; (2) that the Soteria, as reorganized by the Aetolians and superintended by an Aetolian *agonothetes*, were penteteric festivals recurring in the third years of the Olympiad. A subsidiary point is that the pivot from which, working backwards, we have to date the celebrations of the Aetolian Soteria is the archonship of Damokrates in some year earlier than 210 B.C. These issues are not equally certain. The first seems established beyond any reasonable doubt. The second is more controversial. Beloch (*Griech. Gesch.*, IV 2, pp. 385 ff., 489 ff.) maintained that the Soteria were trieteric, but he did so for reasons which are no longer tenable. Dinsmoor contends that the Soteria recurred in the first years of the Olympiad. His grounds are essentially two, that his Tribal Cycles place Polyeuktos in 249/8 B.C., and that Soteria fell in 212 B.C. Neither is compelling. His Tribal Cycles are irreconcilable with the evidence we now possess, and the Soteria of 212 B.C. can be taken to be the annual Amphictyonic fête (*below*, p. 135 ff.). The argument for the date assigned to Damokrates is as follows: *BCH*, 1929, p. 454, no. 38 (Ditt., *Syll.*[3], 538A) is an Amphictyonic decree of Damokrates' year. As is clear from Flacelière's publication, it contained under the heading Αἰτωλῶν the names of only 11 *hieromnemones*, including one, Menekrates, from the Boeotian city Lebadea (Ly . . . . . os and Herias are Delphians). One of the Aetolians is from Kypaira, in Phthiotic Achaia (Stählin, *Das hellenische Thessalien*, pp. 159 ff.). Kypaira was taken from them in 210 B.C. by Philip (Flacelière, *BCH*, 1929, p. 455, n. 1; Dinsmoor, p. 144, n. 1; Holleaux, *CAH*, VIII, pp. 134 f.; Stählin, *Philologus*, 1921, p. 204, *PW*, s.v.). Hence Damokrates is earlier. Besides Menekrates there is another Boeotian *hieromnemon* in the decree of his year (Apollodoros of Tanagra). Hence Damokrates must fall between 217 and 212–211 B.C., or precede 220/19; for Boeotian *hieromnemones* cannot have taken part in a meeting of the Amphictyony at Delphi while the Aetolians were at war with Philip and the Boeotians, as was the case during both the Social War and the First Macedonian War. We shall come back to this argument later (*below*, pp. 120 ff.). The only other clue to the date of Damokrates is that he held office shortly before the Pythia (Ditt., *Syll.*³, 538A).

The records of the Soteria which seem to belong earlier than the archonship of Damokrates, arranged according to the number of the Aetolian *hieromnemones*, are, working backwards, as follows: (11) Flacelière, *BCH*, 1929, p. 456, no. 40 (with 12? *hieromnemones*, partly restored); (10) *idem*, p. 453, no. 37, De . . . tos *agonothetes* (with 13 *hieromnemones*); (9) *BCH*, 1902, pp. 266, 641, no. 17b, ll. 1–4; (8) *BCH*, 1929, p. 453, no. 36, Xennias *agonothetes* (with 15 *hieromnemones*); (7) *idem*, p. 452, no. 35, Charixenos archon, Kallias *agonothetes* (with 14 *hieromnemones*); (6) *idem*, p. 451, no. 33 = *SEG*, II, 260 6, —, son of -adas *agonothetes* (with 14 *hieromnemones*, partly restored); (5) *idem*, p. 451, no. 32 = *SEG*, II, 260 5, Herys archon (with 11 *hieromnemones*); (4) *SEG*, II, 260 4; (3) *SEG*, II, 260 3; (2) Flacelière, *loc. cit.*, p. 449, no. 28 = *SEG*, II, 260 2, Praochos archon (with 9 *hieromnemones*); (1) *SEG*, II, 260 1.[1] Assigning nos. 10-1 (no. 11 may follow Damokrates, since the number of the Aetolian *hieromnemones* is uncertain) to Pythian years preceding 210 B.C., we come at the latest to 250 B.C. with the earliest of these records. On this basis Polyeuktos cannot have come later than 251/0 B.C.; he may, of course, have been four years earlier.

Two difficulties, each of a certain gravity, confront Flacelière's chronology of the Soteria records and involve the date, 255/4 B.C., assigned to Polyeuktos. I should like to state them and suggest possible solutions. In approaching them I am, doubtless, prejudiced in favor of the Tribal Cycles I have now established; but a scrutiny of them from this angle is imperative.

I. Since Dinsmoor's work appeared, the inscription published by Bourguet in *Fouilles de Delphes*, III 1, no. 483 has been identified independently by Robert (*BCH*, 1930, pp. 322 ff.) and Segre (*Historia*, 1931, pp. 241 ff.) as a decree of Smyrna. The identification rests upon the restoration of line 24 as ['Ἀφροδίτῃ τῇ Στρατον]ικίδι, and seems established. The document is the decree of acceptance of the Aetolian Soteria by

[1] According to the evidence of the stones (Dinsmoor, pp. 122 f.), 9 precedes 10 immediately; 7 precedes 8 immediately and both precede 9 either immediately or approximately so; 11 may follow 10 or 8, in either case directly or approximately so, but it cannot follow 8 if it had fewer than 13 Aetolian *hieromnemones*, as seems to be the case; 1-6 succeed in the order of their enumeration, not necessarily in closed sequence throughout. 7 and 8 come from the front, 9 and 10 from the back, and 11 from the right side, of a single block; 1-3 come from the front and 4-6 from the back, of another stone.

Smyrna, and, notwithstanding that it is unique in failing to repeat mechanically the language of the invitation,[1] it is natural to date it at the same time as the similar decrees of Athens (IG^2 II 680), Chios (Ditt., $Syll.^3$, 482), Ios? (*Fouilles de Delphes*, III 1, no. 481; cf. Robert, *BCH*, 1930, p. 323), and Tenos (*idem*, no. 482). It is so badly mutilated as to make a convincing restoration impossible; but since it contains the word "inviolate" ([ἄ]συλον) as well as a reference to Aphrodite Stratonikis, it cannot be disassociated wholly from the documents Ditt., *OGIS*, 229 and 228 and a passage in Tacitus' *Annals* (III, 63), from which it appears that, in obedience to an oracle of Apollo, Seleukos II requested "the kings, dynasts, cities, and *ethne*" to recognize the sanctity and inviolability of the shrine of Aphrodite Stratonikis at Smyrna and the city of Smyrna itself. The Smyrnaeans, Robert thinks, seized the occasion of acceding to the request of the Aetolians to ask in return for themselves the recognition of the sanctity and inviolability of the shrine which they had constructed to harbor the joint cult of Seleukos' father, Antiochos Theos, and grandmother, Stratonike Thea (Ditt., *OGIS*, 229, l. 9), and not only of the shrine but also of the city in which it lay. But Segre calls attention to a difficulty to which this interpretation is subject: it was not Smyrna but Seleukos himself who sent letters to the kings, dynasts, cities, and *ethne*; and in fact it was in response to *his* request that Delphi accorded the

---

[1] Its peculiarities of style are noted by Robert (*BCH*, 1930, p. 327, n. 3), and attributed to the spoken representations of the *theori*. He cites effectively Laqueur, *Epigr. Untersuch. z. d. griech. Volksbeschlüssen*, pp. 32 ff.; see further Herzog, *Hermes*, 1930, pp. 470 f.

desired recognition (Ditt., *OGIS*, 228). It is clear, however, that the Smyrnaeans supported the "letters" of their king by representations of their own (ll. 9 ff.).

The action of Delphi was taken at a time when *theori* were about to depart to announce the Pythia (Ditt., *OGIS*, 228). 246 B.C. was the year of the first Pythia after the accession of Seleukos to the throne; 242 B.C. the year of the second. The conclusion which Robert draws is that the decision of the Aetolians to establish penteteric Soteria was announced to Smyrna (and Athens, Chios, Ios?, and Tenos) in 247/6 or 243/2 B.C., and that in either of these years, certainly after 247 B.C., Polyeuktos was archon in Athens. If this conclusion were accepted, it would seemingly invalidate Dinsmoor's system of Tribal Cycles. My system could be adjusted to it. We should have to move Polyeuktos, Hieron, and Diomedon down a cycle, and (assuming a gap of five years to have intervened between col. i and col. ii of *SEG*, II, 9) date Theophemos, Kydenor, and Eurykleides in 234/3–232/1. The archon-list for the middle of the third century would then have to be constructed as in Table II, Scheme B (pp. 25 f.).

So far as Athens is concerned, 243/2 B.C. is not an inappropriate year for the Aetolians to have extended an invitation to it to accept their Soteria: at that very time they made a treaty with Antigonus envisaging the division between them of the Achaean League (*Polyb.*, II, 43, 10; cf. Plut., *Arat.*, 24; Tarn, *CAH*, VII, p. 734). But in 242 B.C. they could not have approached Sparta or the Achaeans, or Ptolemy, with all of whom they were at war. That was a serious handicap. Seleukos, at war with Ptolemy, was presumably approachable; and so were his cities, Smyrna, for example. The position in the Aegean (Ios?, Tenos, Chios) is obscure. The alternate year, 254 B.C., is singularly appropriate for an appeal by the Aetolians for general recognition of their Soteria. It is the epoch of the second "peace" (see *above*, p. 76), noted exceptionally in the records of the Delian archons (*IG* XI 2, 116, archon Antigonos, — a curious name, — 255 B.C., Durrbach; 254 B.C., Dinsmoor, p. 503), which ended the war between Macedon and Egypt begun in 259/8 B.C., and enabled Antigonus to withdraw his garrison from the Museum. In 254 B.C., so far as we know, the Aetolians were at peace with everybody.

In making an effort to adapt this archon-list to the conclusions already reached we shall have to reëxamine some of them. There is no chance that the beginning of *IG*² II 1534B should be moved down twelve years so as to make the inventory include the two priestly cycles 264/3–241/0 B.C. Quite apart from the "coincidences" which fasten the priesthood of Phileas and Kalliades in 263/2 B.C., there are insuperable obstacles against advancing thus the block of priests furnished by *IG*² II 1534B. In the first place the archon P- would fall in the year of Diognetos; and in the second place we should be unable to find contiguous places for the priest from Xypete (Demetrias, II) and the archon Lysiades mentioned in *IG*² II 775: the priest might be dated in 237/6 B.C., but the archon would have to go down to 230/29 B.C.; yet they should belong to consecutive or approximately consecutive years.[1] Can we

[1] Since the two decrees inscribed on this stone obviously concern two different priests, I do not see how the priest from Xypete honored in the

sustain the position that IG^2 II 1534B included three priestly cycles instead of two, thus beginning in 276/5 B.C. and ending in 241/0 B.C.? To do so, we shall have to abandon the inferences based on the novel phrase in line 297, εἰς τὸν ε- (*above*, p. 40), and assume that the stone contained on the reverse in the neighborhood of 70 lines between that point and the beginning of the account of the commissioners (frg. ρ). On the obverse a correspondingly large surface must have remained blank, since there can be little doubt that IG^2 II 1534A was drawing to a close in line 123. To permit the desired prolongation on the obverse of the stone we should have to assume that the articles in the possession of the priest and the god were entered near the middle of the inventory, and that the list of additional objects was two-thirds the length of the original catalogue. That is highly improbable. It is not a novel opinion that a text thus large or even larger is missing on the reverse. Such had to be assumed to be the case so long as Diomedon was dated in 232/1 B.C. and P- in or about 275/4 B.C. (*Priests of Asklepios*, pp. 131 ff.; Kirchner, IG^2 II iv, pp. 12 ff.). There is, however, an objection to the existence of an extensive blank surface on the obverse, and, consequently, to the lengthening of the inventory on the reverse, which we must consider. It was formulated succinctly by Köhler (IG^1 II 835/6, p. 311) and repeated by Kirchner (IG^2 II 1534B, p. 140): *Uterque scriba vel lapicida rem ita perfecit, ut litteras, quum*

---

first can have served in the archonship of Lysiades, in whose year the second was passed. Yet Dinsmoor's Tribal Cycles force him to put both in the same year (pp. 163 f.).

initio magis inter se distantes incidisset, opera progrediente coartaret. The most natural explanation of this phenomenon is that the stonecutter, becoming anxious lest he should have insufficient space, crowded the letters more closely together as he advanced — a not uncommon procedure. On the reverse the crowding is gradual and progressive, and there is nowhere any sudden narrowing of the space occupied by the letters and their intervals. Moreover, on the completion of his task the stonecutter left uninscribed six cm. of the surface which had been prepared to receive lettering.[1] On the obverse the situation is more complex. The average for letter and space is .0081 in frg. a, .0075 at the beginning of frg. c–l and .0077 at the end. Lines 95–96 and 106–107 are exceptionally crowded (average, .0067).[2] In regard to frg. ρ (which is uninscribed at the bottom on the reverse) Köhler reports that the front is broken away *ut videtur*.[3] Cautiously construed, this evidence is, I believe, negative: the crowding need not have been deliberate on either side. Hence we cannot be certain that a large part of the stone was not left blank at the bottom of the obverse, though the general probabilities are against this supposition.

There are yet other objections to dating Polyeuktos in 243/2 B.C. One has been noted above (p. 35, n. 2):

---

[1] On the reverse a space some $16\frac{1}{2}$ cm. in depth was left for insertion in the socket. It was worked with a small blunt chisel only.

[2] I owe all these measurements to the kindness of Mr. Dow, and the collaboration of Mr. Homer Thompson, Fellow of the American School in Athens.

[3] To test this report the stone would have to be taken out of the cement in which it is now set.

it is not grave.¹ Another is more serious. We become involved in a calendar difficulty. No matter what calendar quality we ascribe to 245/4 B.C. we have a succession of three ordinary or two intercalary years. Fortunately the succession of three ordinary years would come at the end of a Metonic Cycle; and, since a preceding year of this particular cycle (257/6 B.C.) was made intercalary as an afterthought, it is conceivable that a rectification was required later, as in the cycle which included 307/6 B.C. (*above*, p. 5, n. 1).² Furthermore, by dating Polyeuktos in 243/2 B.C. we lose the possibility of operating with two Diomedons and are thus committed definitely to reading the last letter of line four of *IG*² II 791 as a delta. Much more serious are the consequences of so late a date for the chronology of the Delphian records of the Soteria. With Polyeuktos in 243/2 B.C. the Soteria will still fall in the Pythian years; but there is absolutely no possibility of accommodating the records of celebrations of Soteria listed above as nos. 10–1 (p. 111 f.) between the archonship of Damokrates (as commonly dated) and 243/2 B.C., unless we assume one of two things: (1) that there were annual as well as penteteric Soteria at this time and that some of these records deal with the former. They are, however, all alike in form; and all the fêtes were apparently conducted by Aetolian *agonothetae*. It may very well be that there were annual Soteria after the

---

¹ It would become decisive if a re-reading of the stone (which Wilhelm desiderates) should establish Kydenor as the archon-name.

² These are the only unavoidable occurrences of three ordinary years in sequence in the period covered by this monograph; but it should be noted that the calendar quality of many years is conjectural and that in Table II it has been determined throughout to avoid such sequences.

institution of the Aetolian penteteris as well as before, but it seems highly improbable that any of the records we are considering relate to them. The alternate assumption is that the Aetolian Soteria were trieteric.[1] This needs further consideration. There were certainly Amphictyonic Soteria before 254 B.C. (*GDI*, 2646; Ditt., *Syll.*³, 548/9, archon Anaxandridas; cf. *REG*, 1928, p. 85, and n. 3; *BCH*, 1929, p. 272, n. 3).[2] If these were annual, it is conceivable that the Aetolians made them trieteric. It is inconceivable that they were trieteric both before and after the Aetolian reconstruction. What remained for the Aetolians to do in that event? The phrase "every four years" (καθ' ἑκάστην πενταετηρίδα) in the Chian decree of acceptance seems at first sight irreconcilable with a trieteric fête; but Beloch (*Griech. Gesch.*, IV 2, p. 493) has offered an explanation: there was no need for the Chians to appoint *theori* for the Soteria in the Pythian years, since *theori* were already being appointed for that fête, and, alternately, the Soteria were merely its adjunct. It is not a satisfactory explanation (De Sanctis, *Riv. di Fil.*, 1929, p. 572). It leaves Chios without official representation at the Soteria in Pythian years. It is altogether unacceptable if the first appointment of *theori* for the Soteria was made in 242 (or 254) B.C., since 242 was a Pythian year: provision would be lacking for the

[1] On reorganizing the Nikephoria as a trieteric festival (ἰσοπύθιος, ἰσολύμπιος) in 182 B.C. (*BCH*, 1930, p. 333), Eumenes of Pergamon sent out *theori* to secure its acceptance; yet the response of the Aetolians (Ditt., *Syll.*³, 629) does not betray the fact that the fête had been already in existence since a little before 220 B.C. (*Polyb.*, IV, 49, 3; *REA*, 1916, pp. 170 f.), or that it was trieteric (cf. Ditt., *OGIS*, 299).

[2] Anaxandridas precedes Nikodamos.

treating part of Boeotia (including Lebadea) as Aetolian at that time (Pomtow, Ditt., *Syll.*³, 538, n. A), for which there is no evidence. Manifestly we are on insecure ground in dating all Soteria records with 12 Aetolian *hieromnemones* before 210 B.C.

The *terminus ante quem* for an Amphictyonic record with 12 Aetolian *hieromnemones* is, accordingly, the latest possible date for their reduction to 11. To allow room before 198/7 B.C., when our list of definitely ascertained Delphian archons begins (Pomtow, *PW*, IV 2, pp. 2633 ff.; Ditt., *Syll.*³, 585), for the archons Philaitolos and Megartas, we have to make 200/199 B.C. the *terminus ante quem* for this reduction. We can, therefore, place a Soteria record with 12 Aetolian *hieromnemones* in 206 or 202 B.C.; but we cannot place *BCH*, 1929, p. 456, no. 40 in the autumn of 206 B.C., for it contains Boeotian *hieromnemones*, and the election of both Aetolian and Boeotian *hieromnemones* for 206/5 B.C. — the first year after the conclusion of peace between Philip and the Aetolians — occurred after the autumn meeting of the Amphictyonic Council (Dinsmoor, p. 116, n. 1 and *passim*). Let us place it in 202 B.C.; whereupon *BCH*, 1929, p. 458, no. 42 (a Pythian year, archon lacking) may be assigned to 198 B.C. We should thus free 206 B.C. for *BCH*, 1929, p. 453, no. 37 (with 13 Aetolian *hieromnemones*). Should we place it there we could date the first Soteria record in 242 B.C., but we should incur the insuperable obstacle that Boeotian representatives would have to be present in 218 B.C. Nor should we come out much better if we were to date the first Soteria record in 246 B.C.; for this would necessitate an increase of the Aetolian *hieromnemones* from 14 to

15 between 222 and 218 B.C., which seems excluded on historical grounds. Aetolia preserved a strict neutrality between 228 and the outbreak of the Social War (Plut., *Arat.*, 41, 2; *Polyb.*, II, 52, 8; Tarn, *CAH*, VII, pp. 756, 758, 763), in which it lost ground.[1]

We cannot descend below 206 B.C. with an Amphictyonic record containing 13 Aetolian *hieromnemones*. The next possible year is 202 B.C. Between 202 and 198/7 we should have to locate not only Mantias, who is fixed in 200/199 by Livy (XXXI, 32 and *passim*; cf. *GDI*, 2116; Klaffenbach, *op. cit.*, p. L), but also all the Delphian archons in whose years there were 12 or 11 Aetolian *hieromnemones*, namely, Polykleitos, Babylos, Philaitolos, and Megartas — five archons for three years.[2]

On the premises with which we have been working it seems clear that the Aetolian Soteria were created in 251/0 B.C. or earlier. If this is impossible, we shall have to conclude that the Soteria records are only partly penteteric, or that the fête was trieteric and founded in the first year of an Olympiad.

Before accepting a date for Polyeuktos which, besides raising other difficulties, compels us, apparently, to abandon the doctrine that the Aetolian Soteria were

[1] Dinsmoor's arrangement (p. 122) of the records of the Aetolian Soteria (with penteteric festivals recurring in the Olympic years) involves an increase of the Aetolian *hieromnemones* from 14 to 15 between 224 and 220 B.C.

[2] Indeed it will take some manipulation to place a Soteria record with 13 Aetolian *hieromnemones* as late as 206 B.C. We shall have to date the Delphian archons Archelaos (Ditt., *Syll.*³, 534AB; cf. 553a), Alexeas (Ditt., *Syll.*³, 555/6), Euangelos (Ditt., *Syll.*³, 553a, Agetas Aetolian general for the second time), and Hybrias (*GDI*, 2072, 2117; *BCH*, 1881, p. 410, no. 16, Chalepos of Naupaktos Aetolian general) in 212/1–206/5 B.C. This might make trouble (cf. Klaffenbach, *op. cit.*, p. L.)

penteteric, it behooves us to consider closely whether the arguments of Robert for dating *Fouilles de Delphes*, III 1, no. 483 after 247 B.C. are sound. As the response of Smyrna to the invitation of the Aetolians to recognize the Soteria is now deciphered its concluding passage is capable of more than one interpretation. It does not need to be a request of the Smyrnaeans for the recognition of the sanctity and inviolability of the shrine of Aphrodite Stratonikis and their city. It is clear from Ditt., *OGIS*, 229 and 228, as Segre has pointed out (*Historia*, 1931, pp. 245 ff.), that the demand of Seleukos for general recognition of the desired sanctity and inviolability was grounded in an oracle previously received from Apollo in Delphi. This, we can assume, the Smyrnaeans themselves solicited. Consequently, the badly broken lines at the end of *Fouilles de Delphes*, III 1, no. 483 can quite well be taken, with Segre, as instructions given to the *theori*, who were to represent Smyrna at the first celebration of the Aetolian Soteria, to secure an oracle to be used to substantiate the claim of the new (or proposed) shrine and its harboring city to sanctity and inviolability. The use of Delphian oracles in this way is well established, and the oracle can have antedated the achievement of its object by any desired period. The interval in the case of the Magnesian Leukophryena, for example, was as much as 13 years. In support of this interpretation Segre adduces two considerations: (1) the fact already mentioned that it was not the Smyrnaeans but Seleukos who took the measures both at Delphi and elsewhere by which the oracle was put into effect, the weight of which is impaired by the further fact that the Smyrnaeans demonstrably collaborated with the king; and (2) that *Fouilles de Delphes*, III 1, no. 483 was voted before the death of Antiochos II in 247 B.C. This latter consideration would be decisive if it were incontestable. It results from the reading of line 21 of the decree: καὶ βασιλέα Ἀ[ντίοχον]. Had Antiochos been dead he must have been entitled, not King Antiochos, but Theos Antiochos, since the title King belongs to the living ruler in the Seleukid Empire of the third century. We conclude, therefore, that, if the last (defective) letter in line 21 is, as read hitherto, an alpha, we cannot connect the occasion of *Fouilles de Delphes*, III 1, no. 483 with the occasion of Ditt., *OGIS*, 229 and 228 and Tacitus, *Annals*, III, 63.

But as Robert will make clear in a new study which is to appear in the *Revue des études anciennes* and Mr. Dow has ascertained by an examination of the stone at Delphi, the defective letter is not correctly read (cf. Roussel, *REG*, 1932, p. 217). The document belongs after 247 B.C. The only Seleukos who can come in question is Kallinikos. With this reading we cannot avoid attaching the reception of the Aetolian Soteria by Smyrna definitely with his activity in the period following 247 B.C. If the dispatch of his letters synchronized with the request of the Smyrnaeans, and both with the answer given by the Athenians to the Aetolians, Seleukos must have sent off his letters in *ca.* April 1st, 242 B.C. when we make Polyeuktos archon in 243/2 B.C. On this construction Ditt., *OGIS*, 229 must be later; for in it the sending of the letters is ascribed to a past epoch: it seems to coincide with, or follow closely after "the crossing of Seleukos into Seleukis," which Tarn (*CAH*,

VII, p. 718) and Beloch (*Griech. Gesch.*, IV 2, p. 539) agree in placing in 244 B.C. Beloch stresses the fact that Delphi's answer to Smyrna was given shortly before the Pythia;[1] and on the ground, which is more debatable, that Seleukos would not have addressed himself thus to the kings, dynasts, cities, and *ethne* while he was still a pretender, he takes the Pythia to be the celebration of 242 B.C. Can Ditt., *OGIS*, 229 be dated after 242 B.C.? Subsequent to Ptolemy's return from Asia the war was conducted in Syria by his generals and in Asia Minor by his admirals. The peace between the two kings is dated by Tarn (p. 719) in 241 B.C., by Beloch before June 9th, 240 B.C. (Ditt., *OGIS*, 55; Edgar, *Zenon Papyri in the Univ. of Mich. Coll.*, p. 57): it must have been concluded at approximately that time. Hence we might date Ditt., *OGIS*, 229 in 241 or 240 B.C.; whereupon the reference to the dispatch of the letters in the spring of 242 B.C. would be explicable. What coincided with "the crossing of the Tauros by Seleukos" was the loyalty of Smyrna to the pretender. The reward of the king — the grant of autonomy and the dispatch of the letters — came later; how much later we are left to infer. All we know is that it preceded the enactment of Ditt., *OGIS*, 229. Can the attribution to this decree of a date after 242 B.C.

[1] The phrase ἐντείλασται δὲ καὶ τοῖς θεωροῖς -οῖς τὰ Πύθια ἐπαγγελλόντοις doubtless indicates closer proximity to the Pythia than the phrase ἀνειπεῖν τὸν στέφανον τοῦτον τῷ ἀγῶνι τῶν Πυθίων, which, as Flacelière (*BCH*, 1929, pp. 439 f.) points out, was in order, not only in a Pythian year, but in any of the preceding three years. Concordantly, at the time of the Pythia, in the summer of 194 B.C. the Amphictyonic Council instructed the Magnesian *agonothetes* of the Leukophryena to arrange for the proclamation of a crown at this fête though it did not arrive till 192/1 B.C. (Ditt., *Syll.*³, 598B).

be reconciled with the definition of time it contains, νῦν τε ὑπερβεβληκότος τοῦ βασιλέως εἰς τὴν Σελευκίδα? The answer must be in the affirmative. Strictly, this phrase is not a definition of time: it is rather a definition of place. The antithesis is, "formerly the *king* granted autonomy, dispatched letters, etc.": now that the *king* is over the Tauros in Seleukis "his *generals*, zealous to preserve his interests, sent to the military colonists at Magnesia, etc." This they can have done as late as 240 B.C. or as early even as the summer of 242.

The alternate date for the dispatch of the letters, *ca.* April 1st, 246 B.C., would require us to place the crossing of the Tauros by Seleukos in 246 B.C. I do not see why this is absolutely impossible. He can have had the winter of 247/6 B.C. for his preparations. In *ca.* July, 245 B.C. he was recognized as king in Babylon (Clay, *Babylonian Records in the Library of Pierpont Morgan*, II, p. 13, no. 17; Beloch, *Griech. Gesch.*, IV 2, pp. 192, 538). The advance of Ptolemy to the Tigris need not have followed that date: it can have preceded it. On April 12th, 245 B.C. (*Flinders Petrie Papyri*, II, 29e; cf. Edgar, *Zenon Papyri in the Univ. of Mich. Coll.*, p. 57; Dinsmoor, p. 511) prisoners taken by Egypt in the war were already in confinement (Beloch, *Griech. Gesch.*, IV 2, p. 538). The famous campaign in Asia was short (*Catullus*, 66, 35): it can have belonged wholly to the military season of 246 B.C., in which case Euergetes' advance to beyond the Tigris (Ditt., *OGIS*, 54) and back to his own country must have been extraordinarily rapid. Shall we, consequently, date Polyeuktos in 247/6 B.C.? In that case we must conclude that not only are the Soteria records of Delphi non-penteteric at this time, but that Tribal Cycles were not adhered to in Athens. I cannot find this issue tolerable. I should distinctly prefer to date Polyeuktos in 243/2 B.C.

There is a different approach to the problem which it will not do to leave unexplored. It is suggested by the history of the way in which recognition was sought and secured by the Magnesians for the Leukophryena. The command of Apollo (following an epiphany of Artemis) to inaugurate the fête was received in 221/0 B.C. (*Inschr. von Magnesia*, no. 16; Ditt., *Syll.*³, 557). The Magnesians at once solicited the adhesion of the Greek cities of Asia; but this was refused. They let the matter drop for a time. Then they decided to remodel their plans for the *agon* and try again. They approached Athens in 209 B.C. (before the 6th of Pyanopsion, i.e., ca. Nov., *Inschr. von Magnesia*, no. 37; cf. *above*, p. 36, n. 8; Dinsmoor, pp. 208 f.), and doubtless emissaries were at work simultaneously in various parts of the Greek world.[1] In the following year, 208/7 B.C.,[2] the Magnesians record the receipt of favorable responses from the kings

[1] The same *theori* (Apollophanes, Eubulos, and Lykomedes) who visited Athens also visited Chalcis after Philip had been approached (*Inschr. von Magnesia*, no. 47; Ditt., *Syll.*³, 561). Therefore Philip too was solicited, and successfully, in 209/8 B.C., whether before or after Pyanopsion 6th we cannot say. Apollophanes and his two colleagues also visited Eretria, Boeotia, and Phocis (*Inschr. von Magnesia*, nos. 48, 25, 34). The dispatch of *theori* in 209 B.C. to solicit recognition of a fête to be celebrated in 208/7 B.C. is in order. Boesch (Θεωρός, p. 87) estimates that a year was needed by the Magnesian *theori* who toured the Peloponnesus to complete their itinerary.

[2] I take the dating in Ditt., *Syll.*³, 557, l. 25, "in the stephanephorate of Moiragoras, who is the fourteenth from Zenodotos" to be inclusive, as is common in such cases (Dinsmoor, p. 47, n. 3). Accordingly, Moiragoras belongs 13 years after 221/0 B.C., i.e., in 208/7 B.C. It is to be noted that it was in 208/7 B.C. that the answers were received. As the case of Athens shows (*above*, p. 36, n. 8), the *presbeis* were dispatched the previous year.

and Greek cities and *ethne* to which they had sent envoys, and thus they launched their enterprise.[1] The point is that the response from Antiochos III was communicated in 205 B.C. only (*Inschr. von Magnesia*, nos. 18, 19). It was not granted till the return of the king to Antioch in Persis from his great eastern campaign (Holleaux, *CAH*, VIII, p. 142; *BCH*, 1930, pp. 259 f.).[2] We have, accordingly, to reckon in this case with an interval of four years between the general dispatch of *theori* and the receipt of an answer. Can we say that eight or twelve years was an impossibly long interval between the general dispatch of *theori* by the Aetolians and the granting of a favorable response by the Smyrnaeans? I do not think we can. Two Pergamene cities accepted the Leukophryena after the accession of Eumenes to the throne in 197 B.C. (*Inschr. von Magnesia*, nos. 83, 86); two others, among them Tralles (which the Attalids acquired in 188 B.C.), after the accession of Attalos II in 159 B.C. (*Ibid.*, 85, 87). We do not know whether the Aetolians approached Smyrna at the same time that they approached Athens.[3] They may have done so and been unsuccessful. The Greek cities of

---

[1] Accordingly, the fête came in the first years of the Olympiad, the first tentative celebration in 220/19 B.C., Ol. 140, 1 (*Inschr. von Magnesia*, no. 16; Ditt., *Syll.*³, 557), the first generally accepted celebration in 208/7 B.C., Ol. 143, 1.

[2] It is clear from *Inschr. von Magnesia*, no. 61, ll. 42 f. (cf. ll. 100 ff.) that the Greek cities in the basin of the Tigris-Euphrates rivers did not accept the Leukophryena until "many other cities" had already done so. Their solicitation in 205 B.C. was doubtless occasioned by the *epangelia* of the second celebration of the Panhellenic Leukophryena, which was due in 204/3 B.C.

[3] Now that *Fouilles de Delphes*, III 1, no. 481 has been transferred from Teos to one of the Cyclades, probably Ios (Robert, *BCH*, 1930, pp. 323 f.), there is no evidence that any of the cities of Asia recognized the Soteria in the archonship of Polyeuktos.

Asia were capable of refusing such requests. They had doubtless to await the pleasure of their kings before committing themselves financially and politically to the acceptance of a fête like the Soteria.[1] Probably Smyrna did not organize the cult of Aphrodite Stratonikis till after the death of Stratonike in October, 254 B.C. (Tarn, *CAH*, VII, p. 715, n. 1; Segre, *Historia*, 1931, p. 255, n. 36). The temple had then to be built. It was at its completion that *asylia* would naturally be sought for it (Kern, *Inschr. von Magnesia*, p. 13, note). Seleukos may have taken the matter in hand in 246 B.C., or he may have waited till 242 B.C. when he was in possession of his kingdom. As a *quid pro quo* to the Aetolians the Smyrnaeans may have thought it good policy to accept the Soteria, either in compliance with a

[1] In general it seems to be an unfounded assumption that festivals, newly founded or reorganized, were accepted by all rulers and peoples simultaneously. Such was certainly not the case with the festival of Hekate founded by Stratoniceia in 81 B.C. (Ditt., *OGIS*, 441, ll. 140 ff.). The *asylia* of Teos was also recognized by different states at different times and by various Cretan cities twice (*GDI*, 5165–5180; 5181–5187). Even if its recognition by the Delphian Amphictyony and the Delphians (Ditt., *Syll.*[3], 564, 565, Megartas archon), and by the Aetolians (Ditt., *Syll.*[3], 563, Alexander of Kalydon general) and the Athamanes (Le Bas-Waddington, *Voyage archéologique*, III, 83; *GGA*, 1898, p. 217) can be dated in the same year (201 B.C.) as its acceptance by the Cretan cities (Holleaux, *Klio*, 1913, pp. 137 ff.),— a controversial question, — the Romans did not take action till 193 B.C. (Ditt., *Syll.*[3], 601). The normal thing was for the general appeal, when it seemed well grounded or was supported by influential persons, such as kings or their representatives (Holleaux, *loc. cit.*), to be followed immediately by a large group of acceptances, and at intervals thereafter by straggling adhesions, dependent upon accidental or political circumstances. It seems clear, moreover, from *Inschr. von Magnesia*, nos. 18, 19, 22, 47 and 61 that the Magnesians did not, or could not, approach the cities subject to a monarch without first approaching him and securing from him the emission of letters either to his cities directly, or to the appropriate royal officials, indicating his pleasure in the matter.

recent request that they should do so (Delphian *theori* announcing the Pythia were in Smyrna in 246 and 242 B.C.), or in belated response to an invitation sent to them by Charixenos in 254 B.C. In any event the original decree of the Aetolians would naturally be the basis of action, just as it was in response to the original decree of the Magnesians that Antiochos III acted in 205 B.C. We may attribute the acceptance thus tardily by Smyrna of the Aetolian Soteria to a change of Seleukid policy coincident with the change, in such exceptional circumstances, of ruler;[1] or to the conclusion of the Smyrnaeans that if they wanted something from Delphi they would do well to conciliate the Aetolians.

If we accept the solution of the problem which this method of approach suggests, we can leave Polyeuktos in 255/4 B.C., and maintain the conclusion that the Aetolian Soteria were penteteric. And since the wording of the Chian decree of acceptance (*above*, pp. 109, 119 f.), which obviously synchronized with the Athenian decree, excludes a trieteric fête founded in the only other year (242 B.C.) permitted by the Tribal Cycles, this is the solution which I prefer.

[1] We do not know definitely when the Second Syrian War, between Ptolemy II and Antiochos II, ended. Tarn (*CAH*, VII, p. 714) thinks that it, as well as the war between Ptolemy II and Antigonus, terminated in 255 B.C. Edgar (*Zenon Papyri in the Univ. of Mich. Coll.*, p. 4), following Otto (*Abh. Bay. Akad.*, 34, 1928, p. 46; cf. *Philologus*, 1931, pp. 416 ff.), affirms that it was closed in 253 B.C. at the latest. The marriage between Ptolemy's daughter, Berenike, and Antiochos was consummated early in 252 B.C.; that between Antiochos' sister (Tarn, *CAH*, VII, p. 715, n. 1), Stratonike, and Antigonus' son, Demetrius, in 253 or 252 (Dinsmoor, p. 498). If Antiochos was left out of the "peace" of 255 B.C., and was consequently forced to continue the war with Ptolemy unaided, he was doubtless in no mood in 254 B.C. to confer a favor on the Aetolians, who were at that time protégés of Macedon (Tarn, *CAH*, VII, p. 217).

II. The second of the two difficulties mentioned above (p. 112) is of a different character. It involves the vexed question of the relations of the Egyptian and the Macedonian months in the calendar of the Ptolemies which Dinsmoor (Appendix G, pp. 471 ff.) and Edgar (*Zenon Papyri in the Univ. of Mich. Coll.*, pp. 50 ff.) have discussed most recently. I feel incompetent to trace to the sources the divergences of their results (Dinsmoor makes 245 B.C. intercalary, Edgar ordinary); and do not feel called upon to do so, since they seem immaterial to the question with which I am concerned. This is the interpretation of the well-known funerary inscription from Alexandria which was first published by Merriam (*AJA*, 1885, pp. 22 ff.), and from which we learn that Sotion, the son of Kleon, of Delphi, θεωρὸς τὰ Σωτήρια ἐπαγγέλλων, was buried by Theodotos, the *agorastes*, in the ninth year of some Ptolemy. The ninth year (regnal) of Ptolemy III was 238/7 B.C. (April 1st to March 19th, Dinsmoor; Feb. 26th to Feb. 14th, Edgar). Since the Soteria were celebrated in August–September 238 B.C., on Flacelière's chronology, this would suit admirably. But in the ninth year of the same Ptolemy (Theodotos is again *agorastes*) Hyperberetaios 30th fell on Pharmouthi 7th (Pagenstecher, *AJA*, 1909, p. 408, no. 22), that is to say, Dios 1st equalled Pharmouthi 8th. But in the ninth regnal year of Euergetes Thoth 1st was Oct. 22d (238 B.C.) and consequently Pharmouthi 8th was May 27th (238 B.C.); whereas Dios 1st of his ninth regnal year was Feb. 25th (237 B.C.), according to Dinsmoor (pp. 479, 491), or, according to Edgar (*op. cit.*, p. 56), Jan. 22d (237 B.C.). The discrepancy (eight or nine months) is irreconcilable. We could reduce it to two months 19 days, or three months 25 days by equating Pharmouthi 8th of the ninth regnal year with Dios 1st of the eighth year, which fell on March 8th, 238 B.C. (Dinsmoor, p. 479), or on Feb. 2d (Edgar). But even so the dates of the two calendars are much too far apart to be synchronized by anything short of a revolutionary change in current determinations of the positions of the Macedonian months. On the other hand, the ninth year of Philopator can be made to fit the synchronism on the assumption that Philopator came to the throne on Sept. 13th, 222 B.C. by the further assumption that Theodotos dated the regnal years by the Macedonian calendar (Dinsmoor, p. 491). On the assumption that Philopator came to the throne in 221 B.C. (July 28th, Beloch, *Griech. Gesch.*, IV 2, p. 495; Tarn, *CAH*, VII, p. 864), it will fit without this second assumption. Apparently no other Ptolemy comes in question (Dinsmoor, p. 491). On the basis of the current determinations of the Ptolemaic calendar, the ninth year of Philopator seems fixed for the *epangelia* of the Soteria by Sotion. The year, on Dinsmoor's showing, is 213/2 B.C., thus bringing the celebration of the Soteria he announced into 212 B.C. (Ol. 142, 1). This suits his dating of Polyeuktos in 249/8 B.C. But the matter is complicated by the fact that we have to do in Ptolemaic Egypt with datings reckoned from different epochs. There were, for example, regnal years computed from one point (the accession day of the king) and fiscal years computed from another point (the preceding Mecheir 1st). It thus happens, on Dinsmoor's system, that Pharmuthi 7th of the ninth fiscal year of Philopator falls on May 20th, 214 B.C. If this was the date of Sotion's death, he can have been present in Alexandria to announce the penteteric Soteria of the following midsummer. We should encounter a difficulty, however, in that, on this synchronism, Dios 1st (May 21st) would fall 12 days after the new moon (May 9th, Athens). Beloch (*Griech. Gesch.*, IV 2, p. 42) abandons the attempt to make the Macedonian months jibe with the lunar periods when he comes to the reign of Philopator; by using (where discrepancies would occur otherwise) years numbered from the first New Year's Day of the Macedonian calendar after the accession of Philopator, Dinsmoor is able to construe the Macedonian months of Philopator's reign as true lunar months. If he is right and the lunar months must coincide with the lunar periods, the ninth year of the Sotion document cannot be the fiscal year.

There is yet a further possibility to be considered. The year in question may be the ninth year of Euergetes and the day the 7th of Pharmouthi (May 26th, 238 B.C.), and its equation with Hyperberetaios 30th (Feb. 24th or Jan. 21st, 237; March 8th or Feb. 2d, 238 B.C.) be incorrect. As Edgar points out (*op. cit.*, p. 52), "most of the Greeks in the χώρα (even the ὑποδιοικητής, and the οἰκονόμος, though not the στρατηγός or the military in general) used the more convenient Egyptian calendar for ordinary purposes and could not have given the Macedonian date without difficulty. So long as Zenon's headquarters were in Alexandria, he used the Macedonian calendar only, but after coming to Philadelphia, be began to double-date his dockets, in imitation of his master (Apollonios). He found it difficult;

after a short time he gave up the attempt to keep an exact concordance, and either assimilated the Macedonian to the Egyptian month or placed one ten days in front of the other (see *P. Cairo Zen.*, vol. 2, index 4); and after two years of this unsatisfactory procedure he gave up the Macedonian calendar altogether." If the year were the ninth of Euergetes, instead of Hyperberetaios 30th Theodotos should have written Peritios 26th (Edgar). Instead of the fourth Macedonian month he wrote the twelfth. He cannot have been thus far off by an error of computation or by any vagary of correlation. Moreover, Theodotos was an official, not of the χώρα, but of the court. The possibility exists, however, that he also failed "to keep an exact concordance"; whereupon we could date the burial of Sotion on May 20th, 214 B.C. (7th Pharmouthi of the ninth fiscal year of Philopator), regarding the resulting discrepancy of 12 days between his Dios 1st and the true lunation as due to his arbitrary system of concordances.

On the other hand, should we accept 212 B.C. as the year of the *epangelia* of the Soteria by Sotion, since it is unlikely that he died two years before the celebration he was to announce or two years after the celebration he had announced, we can assume with Segre (*Historia*, 1931, p. 256, n. 40) that the Soteria he came to announce were the annual Soteria (Flacelière, *BCH*, 1928, pp. 269 ff.).[1] It can be thought surprising that *theori* were sent so far afield to announce this minor fête, but we do not know what the practice of the Amphictyony was in this matter: it had a very highly organized sys-

---

[1] The objection of Beloch (*Griech. Gesch.*, IV 2, p. 494, cf. Dinsmoor, p. 126) to Pomtow's restoration of *Inschr. von Magnesia*, no. 91 (Ditt., *Syll.*³,

tem of *theori* and *theorodoki* (*BCH*, 1921, pp. 1 ff.); and prior to 254 B.C., when the Soteria were certainly annual, *theori* were sent abroad to announce them (Ditt., *Syll.*³, 398, 549). Moreover, the political situation of the Aetolians in 212 B.C., on the eve of the First Macedonian War, was such that they may have sought, by sending special *theori* to Alexandria, either alone or accompanied by political envoys, to sound the court of Ptolemy on the approaching struggle. The interest of Egypt in the war that ensued is well attested. Of course, if the Aetolian Soteria were trieteric, the fête might conceivably fall in 212 B.C.; but since the fête, if trieteric, could not have been founded in a Pythian year (*above*, pp. 119 ff.), it would not fall in 212 B.C.

The general conclusions which accord best with the facts in our possession are, accordingly, that the Aetolian Soteria were founded in 254 B.C. in the archonship of Hieron; that they were accepted by Seleukos II and his cities only in 242 B.C.; that they were a penteteric fête recurring in the Pythian years; and that after 254 B.C. the annual Soteria founded by the Amphictyony in 278 B.C. continued to be celebrated in the non-Pythian years. These conclusions involve the acceptance of the archon- and secretary-list drawn up in Scheme A, Table II.

598; *SEG*, III, 386), ll. 10 f., ἀναγορεῦσαι δὲ τὸν [στέφανο]ν Σωτηρίοις - - καθ' ἕκασ[τον ἐνιαυτόν], is not tenable. Es ist doch klar (he affirms), dass eine solche Bekränzung nicht Jahr für Jahr ausgerufen sein kann. Yet in IG^2 II 212 (347/6 B.C.) provision was made for crowning Spartokos and Pairisades at each successive Great Panathenaia (Kirchner, note; *Treasurers of Athena*, p. 134, n. 3), and in Michel, *Recueil*, 1016, ll. 15 ff. the annual announcement of a crown is prescribed. Cf. for further examples Wilhelm, *Sitz. wien. Akad.*, 214, 4 (1932), pp. 16 ff.

PART II

THE SECOND CENTURY B.C. AND AFTER

PART II

THE SECOND CENTURY B.C. AND AFTER

XI. THE CRISIS OF 201/0 B.C.

THE view expressed tentatively above (p. 20) that "Dinsmoor's Tribal Cycles between 228 B.C. and the time of Sulla may be right even if the new evidence regarding Diomedon and Ekphantos requires us to reject his secretary-cycle between 262/1 and 229/8 B.C." has had to be modified: we have seen that his Tribal Cycles between 228 and 201/0 B.C. stand or fall with his Tribal Cycles between 262/1 and 229/8 B.C. It remains to determine whether his Tribal Cycles between 201/0 and 145/4 B.C., when we reach firm ground, are tenable. Since I have to postulate a break in the secretary-cycle in 201/0 B.C., the two cycles, his and mine (no third system is possible), must be considered on their merits. Since his set of cycles precedes mine by one year only, the difference for purposes of historical chronology is slight. It has, however, considerable significance for the doctrine of Tribal Cycles.

In 138/7 B.C. (Timarchos archon) the secretary came from Kekropis (VIII) and the priest from Ptolemais (V). Again, probably in 114/3 B.C., the secretary and priest were from these same *phylae*. In Pelops' archonship (166/5 or 165/4 B.C.), on the other hand, the secretary was from Ptolemais (V) and the priest from Erechtheis (I). To bring these data into harmony we must assume that between 166/4 B.C. and 138/7 a dislocation of one *phyle* occurred. The question is, which of the two cycles was disturbed? Dinsmoor brings into the problem the conceded irregularity in the secretary rotation in 146/5 B.C., where the secretary is from Kekropis (VIII) when he should have been from Antiochis (XI), and opts for the continuity of the priestly cycle of Asklepios. He thus places Pelops in 166/5 B.C. and a priest from Pandionis in 200/199 B.C. to follow a priest from Aigeis in 201/0 B.C.

But it is conceded that there is a discontinuity in the priestly cycle of Asklepios in 109 B.C. It is conceivable, therefore, that there was another between 166/4 and 138 B.C.; and now that we have seen that the *phyle* to hold the priesthood in 201/0 B.C. was not Aigeis, but Antiochis, we should have to assume, on accepting Dinsmoor's cycles for the second century and rejecting them for the third, that there was an inexplicable jump in the priestly cycle from Antiochis to Aigeis or (attributing both parts of 201/0 B.C. to Antiochis) to Pandionis in 201–200 B.C.; and similarly in the case of the secretary, we should have to assume that the transition was without reason, — from Aiantis to Akamantis or Oineis. Let us put Pelops as hitherto in 165/4 B.C. (that is to say, Xenokles in 168/7; see *above*, p. 11 n. 1). Then working back from the tribal relations of secretary and priest in that year (V : I) we arrive in 201/0 B.C. with a secretary from Ptolemais and a priest from Erechtheis. We know that it was after the time of the Mysteries in 201/0 B.C. (Boedromion) that the two *phylae*, Antigonis and Demetrias, were abolished. It is, therefore, permissible to believe that the priest for the first part of the year 201/0 B.C. was taken from Antiochis, and that for the second part of the year he was chosen from Erechtheis.[1] Thus our priestly cycle of Asklepios runs: 202/1, Aiantis; 201/0, Antiochis; 201/0 (second part), Erechtheis; 200/199, Aigeis. We have then to note that, whereas in 263/2 B.C. the priest for the second part of the year came from the same *phyle* as the one for the first part, in 201/0 B.C. the second

[1] The mere fact of the redistribution of the demes into eleven *phylae* (IG^2 II 2362) shows that some little time elapsed between the abrogation of Antigonis and Demetrias and the creation of Attalis. The abrogation cannot have antedated the rupture of relations between Athens and Philip. This was a consequence of Macedonian participation in the Acarnanian devastation of Attica (*Livy*, XXXI, 14, 6–10). Holleaux (*CAH*, VIII, p. 161) dates the invasion early in 200 B.C., immediately after Philip's return from Asia. The interval during which eleven *phylae* can have existed was, on this chronology, very short indeed, since Holleaux dates the creation of Attalis (*Polyb.*, XVI, 25; *Livy*, XXXI, 15) in *ca.* May, 200 B.C. (*ibid.*, p. 162): Antigonis and Demetrias, he adds, "seemingly had just been abolished." After the creation of Attalis Philip raided and raged in Attica, and in retaliation the Athenians (autumn of 200 B.C.) passed a decree of outlawry against him and his house (*Livy*, XXXI, 44, 2). Had the abolition of Antigonis and Demetrias formed part of the act of outlawry (thus dated), it would have followed the creation of Attalis; and, in consequence, Athens would have had, not eleven *phylae*, but fourteen *phylae* in 200 B.C. This, however, is impossible. IG^2 II 2362 began with a list of the demes of Erechtheis, not of Antigonis (Schoeffer, *PW*, V, p. 32; Tod, *Annual of the British School in Athens*, 1902/3, pp. 173 ff.; Dinsmoor, p. 451, n. 1; Kirchner, note).

The rupture of Athens and Macedon, i.e., the Acarnanian incident, can perfectly well have occurred before the return of Philip from Asia: he did not himself lead the Macedonian troops which coöperated with the Acarnanians. The *terminus post quem* is the celebration of the Eleusinian Mysteries in Boedromion (September), 201 B.C. Before that date we have no evidence of bad relations between Athens and Philip (Holleaux, *Rome, la Grèce et les monarchies hellénistiques*, pp. 265 ff.). I should date the Acarnanian raid and the abrogation of Antigonis and Demetrias in the autumn of 201 B.C. The nature of the Athenian reaction is intelligible when it is recalled that for the first time since 229 B.C. the neutrality of Athens had been violated.

priest came from the *phyle* next in order. But we have
at least one parallel for the practice conjectured in
201/0 B.C. In 411/0 B.C. Erechtheis furnished the secretary of the *tamiae* for the first two months, Antiochis for
the following ten (*Treasurers of Athena*, pp. 9, 147), in
accordance with the reverse of the official order then
used (*ibid.* p. 143, n. 2). Moreover, what the situation
called for in 263/2 B.C. was simply a change in the personnel of administration. There was then no alteration
in the composition of the *phylae* to warrant a change
of the priest to a new *phyle*. In 201/0 B.C. the situation was altogether different. Antigonis and Demetrias
were abolished and their demes returned to the *phylae*
from which they had been taken in 307/6 B.C. The
restoration of these demes (24 at least in number) altered the personnel of all the ten original tribes, except
Aiantis (Dinsmoor, p. 450), and enabled demesmen of
Antigonis and Demetrias, thus distributed, to secure
the offices, rotating by *phylae*, at every allotment.
The shuffle of the demes called for a new deal of the
tribes. In the case of the priesthood of Asklepios the
phyle in office when the shuffle was made happened to
be Antiochis. By choosing the one next in sequence
(Erechtheis) to begin the new cycle discontinuity in
this Tribal Cycle was avoided. Here the choice was
easy. In the case of the prytany-secretariat the choice
was not thus predetermined. At the time of the shuffle
this office was held by Aiantis. As can be seen from a
glance at Table II, the *phyle* which began the new cycle
was Ptolemais. I think that in the circumstances the
choice was a natural one. In 224/3 B.C. the *phyle*
which bore the name of the Egyptian dynasty was not

singled out for any special consideration: it secured offices only when its turn came round, not sooner. Now an occasion has arisen to make amends. Ptolemais was the only *phyle* (except Aiantis itself) from which demes were not subtracted or to which demes were not added by the shuffle (Dinsmoor, p. 451). Its personnel, accordingly, remained unaffected by the reconstructive measures necessitated by the abolition of the two Macedonian *phylae*. It alone stood ready for immediate use. Since, however, various offices began cycles in the official order in the course of 201/0 B.C., and they were doubtless distributed horizontally by tribes, the general assignment of officials was probably delayed till all eleven *phylae* were ready to make appointments. There may have been exceptional need for immediate action in the case of the prytany-secretaryship, without which no business could be transacted by Council or Ecclesia.[1] But we shall probably be on safer ground in attributing the choice of Ptolemais for this office to the desire of the Athenians to honor Ptolemy. There can be no doubt that between 224 and 201/0 B.C. Ptolemy was almost the official protector of the neutrality of Athens. Polybius (V, 106, 6–8; cf. *Livy*, XXXI, 9, 1) implies as much. He tells us with unmistakable rancor that "following the policy and inclinations of their

---

[1] The procedure followed in 307/6 B.C. is interesting in this connection. In order to satisfy two desires, (1) to avoid discontinuity in the secretariat, and (2) to honor Poliorcetes by giving this office to his *phyle*, the deme of Diomeia was transferred from Aigeis to Demetrias notwithstanding that Aigeis belonged to the group of *phylae* which was to furnish demes to Antigonis (Dinsmoor, p. 450 and n. 3; cf. *above*, p. 64, n. 1). Lysias of Diomeia was thus enabled to be secretary for the entire year. This case shows that the secretaryship might be treated as an exception.

leading statesmen Eurycleides and Micion, the Athenians took no part in the affairs of the rest of Greece, but were profuse in their adulation of all the kings, and chiefly of Ptolemy, consenting to every variety of decree and proclamation however humiliating, and paid little heed to decency in this respect owing to the lack of judgement of their leaders" (Translation by Paton in the *Loeb Classics*). The extant inscriptions confirm his account of the Egyptian orientation of the foreign policy of Eurykleides and Mikion (*Hell. Ath.*, pp. 239, 241 ff., 267 ff.; Holleaux, *CAH*, VIII, p. 129). On their embroilment with Philip in 201/0 B.C. the Athenians invoked the aid of Ptolemy, as well as of Attalos, Rhodes, Aetolia, and some Cretan towns (*Paus.*, I, 36, 5 f.; *Livy*, XXXI, 9); and whatever may have been the relations of Agathokles and his clique with Philip at the moment (Holleaux, *CAH*, VIII, pp. 150 ff.), there is every likelihood that they were profuse with promises to Athens. They could undertake to use their good offices with Philip if they were still conducting friendly negotiations with him on their own account. Athens did not commit itself to the Roman-Pergamene-Rhodian program till the time of the creation of Attalis in 200 B.C. It should be remarked that the creation of Attalis offered no more occasion for disrupting the priestly and secretary-cycles than did the creation of Ptolemais. The subtracting of demes from the old *phylae* (Ptolemais was again undisturbed) for the building up of a new one had no such consequences on the personnel of the tribes generally as the abolition of Antigonis and Demetrias (cf. *above*, pp. 95 f., 142).

XII. The Secretary-cycle with Allotted Order of *Phylae*, 157/6–146/5 b.c.

Beginning with Ptolemais in 201/0 b.c. the secretary-cycles were maintained till the "dictatorship" of Argeios in 97/6 b.c., and probably till the "dictatorship" of Medeios in 91/0–89/8 b.c. (Dinsmoor, p. 33, and Table II, *above*, pp. 28 ff.). But, as already pointed out, between 160/59 (Tychandros archon) and 145/4 b.c. (Metrophanes archon) a deviation from the official order occurred. The secretary for the archonship of Epikrates belonged to Kekropis (VIII) when he should have belonged to Antiochis (XI). Two explanations of this anomaly are presentable: (1) that Epikrates is incorrectly dated in 146/5 b.c.; and (2) that for the cycle between 157/6 and 146/5 b.c. (inclusive) the twelve *phylae* held the secretariat in an allotted, and not in the official order. For the former something could once be said (*Class. Phil.*, 1913, pp. 220 ff.), when we had only Plassart's text of the list of Delian gymnasiarchs (*BCH*, 1912, pp. 395 ff.); but it has had to be withdrawn in view of the more correct publication subsequently made by Roussel (*Délos*, pp. 196 ff.). The view cannot longer be sustained that the order of the names in this list was not chronological throughout (Dinsmoor, pp. 229 ff.): it was such when it can be tested, and, except for 141/0 b.c. when there were two gymnasiarchs (*below*, p. 172),[1] there is precisely one

---

[1] Plassart (*BCH*, 1912, pp. 399 f.), on first publishing the list, urged that Aristomenes, the gymnasiarch with whom it begins, served in 166/5 b.c., and that the twenty-sixth and twenty-seventh names belonged to a single year. His arguments were met by Roussel (*ibid.*, p. 400; cf. *Délos*, pp. 343 ff.)

name for each year from 166/5 B.C., "when Athens regained the island through the Romans" (ἀφ' οὗ διὰ Ῥωμαίων ἀνεκτήσατο τὴν νῆσον), to the termination of the catalogue in 112/1 B.C. We have, therefore, to fall back upon the second explanation.[1] In its favor it can be urged that in 145/4 B.C. the cycle continues as if it had never been interrupted, thus suggesting that, whatever their order may have been, all the *phylae* held in turn the secretariat in the interval during which the official order was disturbed. In view of earlier practice (*above*, pp. 49 ff.), it is natural to conclude that the period of deviation from the fixed order was one whole cycle. It cannot have been two: the official order was being observed in 161–159 B.C. and again in 145/4. Why the Athenians should have decided to adopt in 157/6 B.C. the practice of allotting the secretariat to the *phylae* in turn we do not know. To allot the *phylae* year after

---

by counter arguments of which I have admitted the force (*Class. Phil.*, 1913, p. 220). But Dinsmoor (pp. 229 ff.) has now sustained Plassart's position by reasons which seem to me decisive.

[1] By dating Xenokles in 169/8 B.C. Dinsmoor is precluded from using this explanation. He has also to place Achaios in 167/6 B.C. In this year the Athenian financial regime already existed on Delos (Roussel, *Délos*, p. 351, n. 1). It is possible that the Athenian officials put in charge of the Sacred Money assumed office before Hekatombaion, 166 B.C., when gymnasiarchs were first installed; but in 157/6 B.C. they began their term of service later, in Metageitnion (*below*, p. 166 ff.). The current explanation, that they first entered upon their duties in the middle of the year 167/6 B.C. (at the beginning of the Delian year 166 B.C., on Gamelion 1st, Attic), and advanced their inaugural date to Metageitnion by 157/6 B.C., is far from satisfactory (Roussel, *Délos*, p. 140, n. 1). It encounters the obstacle that in the earliest Delian inventory which has reached us (*ibid.*, pp. 126 ff.) *une transmission partielle est faite en Hékatombaion*, on Hekatombaion 7th, to be exact. The view is tenable that an Areopagite commission, for which see Roussel (*Délos*, p. 127), inaugurated the financial regime of Athens on the

year, as the prytanies were allotted prytany after prytany, or to draw lots for all twelve *phylae* at the beginning of the cycle and stick to the order thus determined, required some additional effort and mechanism; but the consequences on tribal representation in office were nil.

XIII. CONSTITUTIONAL CRISES OF 103–88 B.C.

I ACCEPT without reservations Dinsmoor's dating of the archon-group, Theokles-Herakleitos (IG^2 II 2336), in 103/2–96/5 B.C., instead of 102/1–95/4 B.C. It agrees with my own earliest attribution (*Athenian Archons*, pp. 86 f.), subsequently withdrawn (*Priests of Asklepios*, p. 144) in deference to the arguments of Kirchner (*GGA*, 1900, pp. 473 ff.) and Kolbe (*Die attischen Archonten*, p. 137). With it falls my contention that in 103/2 B.C. a revolution occurred in Athens of which the alleged break of the official order in that year was taken to furnish the proof. If I understand him aright, Dinsmoor denies the reality of any drastic alteration in the political institutions of Athens in this general epoch. There I cannot follow him. Between 106/5 B.C. (IG^2 II 1011, l. 42) and 101/0 (IG^2 II 1028)[1] a change of serious

---

island, and that it was not till some time after Hekatombaion 1st, 166 B.C., that the regular board of commissioners of *Hiera* and Sacred Funds took charge. However that may be, if the archon-names, Achaios and Pelops, are significant in the sense indicated above (pp. 86 f.), Achaios cannot have been elected to the archonship at the elections for 167/6 B.C.; for at that time Delos had not yet been awarded to the Athenians.

[1] During this same epoch a reorganization of the Delphian Pythais and a new organization of the Delian Pythais occurred. The famous list of first fruits brought to Apollo Pythios by Delian and Athenian officials (IG^2 II 2336) covers the eight years from Theokles to Herakleitos (103/2–96/5 B.C.).

import took place (cf. *Klio*, 1904, pp. 1 ff.; *Hell. Ath.*, p. 427, n. 4). In the former year, as on all earlier occasions (IG^2 II 1006, l. 88, 122/1 B.C.; 1008, l. 61, 118/7 B.C.; 1009, l. 45, 116/5 B.C.), the *kosmetes* "stood his audit in the dicastery, as required by law, for all his acts during his magistracy" (περὶ πάντων τῶν κατὰ τὴν

It ended at the completion of the enneeteris, which thus ran from Ol. 169, 2 to Ol. 171, 1. The decision to collect the first fruits and send the Pythais was made by popular vote (IG^2 II 2336, preamble), obviously in 103 B.C. As to whether the Pythais of IG^2 II 2336 is the well-known Pythais sent to Delphi, as Colin (*Le culte de Apollon Pythien à Athènes*, pp. 134 ff.) maintains, or an otherwise unknown Pythais sent to Delos, as Kirchner (note, p. 688) upholds, needs further investigation. In favor of the former opinion is cited the phrase of *Fouilles de Delphes*, III 2, no. 48, τὰν ἱερὰν νομιζομέναν Πυθαΐδα δι' ἐννεετηρίδος πεμψάντων 'Αθηναίων. Colin dates the document containing this phrase in the first archonship of Argeios. Now that Dinsmoor (pp. 240 ff.) has fixed this archonship in 98/7 (Ol. 170, 3), it appears that the Pythais of Agathokles' archonship (Ol. 169, 3) occupied an enneeteric relation with that of Argeios' year. Hence we should infer that the decision to send the Pythais to Delphi δι' ἐννεετηρίδος was taken in 106 B.C. (cf. *Fouilles de Delphes*, III 2, pp. 291 f.). The epigraphical facts permit us to reverse the dates assigned by the French editor to *Fouilles de Delphes*, III 2, nos. 48 and 49, thus dating the latter in 98/7 and the former in 106/5 B.C. This was proved by Boethius in his excellent monograph (*Die Pythaïs*, Uppsala, 1918, pp. 92 ff.).

The objections of Kirchner to interpreting the Pythais of IG^2 II 2336 as Delphian have considerable force. He points out that the official in charge of the first fruits of the Delphian Pythais in 106/5 B.C. was Amphikrates, whereas the official who had the like charge in IG^2 II 2336 was . . . . ates, his brother (Eukrates or Epikrates) probably; and that, whereas . . . . ates is designated in IG^2 II 2336 as in charge for the entire enneeteris (103/2–96/5 B.C.), the Delphian Pythais of 98/7 B.C. was in charge of Sarapion of Melite. The participation of the priests at Delos alone in the collections recorded in IG^2 II 2336 is decisive. Had it been the Delphian Pythais that was involved the priests at Athens must have contributed. It is also significant in this sense that the hipparchs and the ephebe officials are absent and that three "generals" ἐπὶ τὸ ναυτικόν are present. A sending over sea, and not by land, was obviously contemplated. I conjecture that the three sacred triremes

ἀρχὴν ἔδωκεν τὰς εὐθύνας ἐν τῷ δικαστηρίῳ κατὰ τὸν νόμον). In IG^2 II 1028 (101/0 B.C.) this significant fact is omitted.[1] It is there recorded (ll. 89 ff.) "he held a review of the ephebes in the presence of the Council and presented to that body a defense of his official acts and of everything that occurred in the course of the year relating to the ephebes" (ἐποιήσατο δὲ καὶ τὴν ἀπόδειξιν αὐτῶν καὶ τὸν ἀπολογισμὸν ἐν τῇ βουλῇ ὑπὲρ τῶν κατὰ τὴν ἀρχὴν καὶ περὶ τῶν ἐν τῷ ἐνιαυτῷ γεγονότων πάντων τοῖς ἐφήβοις). The review was old (IG^2 II 1006, l. 33; 1008, l. 29; 1011, l. 21); the defense before the Council was new. A justificatory statement to the Council was substituted for the public examination before the jury-court thereto-

---

carried the Pythais to the island and that Archias of Anaphlystos, the "general" ἐπὶ τὸ ναυτικόν, whose name is blazoned in huge letters in lines 255 f., had general supervision of the transport (cf. *Klio*, 1909, pp. 314 ff.).

Assuming the Pythais to have been Delian, it was sent for the first time in 96/5 (Ol. 171, 1), when the first fruits for the enneeteris were all collected. It was in this year alone, it may be noted, that officials for back years paid their scot. The second Pythais was accordingly due in 88/7 B.C., and the ill-fated expedition of Apellikon in that year may have been its escort, formally at least, seeing that Posidonios scoffs at its chief for behaving more like one conducting a panegyris than an army (*Athen.*, V, 214 f.). There seem to be no traditional motives for sending the Pythais to Delos in the first years of the Olympiad unless it be that in the Delian hepteteris mentioned by Aristotle (*Ath. Pol.*, 54, 7) the fête, spaced with reference to the Delia (which then came in the third years of the Olympiad), was held in the first years of Olympiads at intervals of eight and four years alternately, thus *1 2 3 4 1 2 | 3 4 *1 2 3 4 | *1 2 3 4 1 2 | .

[1] Bruno Keil's warning (*Ber. d. Gesell. d. Wiss. zu Leipzig*, 71, 1919, p. 27) that inferences from the formulas of decrees are invalid at this time because documents were often published privately (hence inexactly) does not apply in a case of this sort. The publication of all these decrees was imposed, as in earlier times, upon the prytany-secretary. Keil (*op. cit.*, p. 64) is doubtless right in thinking that private suits came, as theretofore, before the dicasteries.

fore required by law. Because of the defective character of our sources the alteration of the law is demonstrable only for this one magistrate; but it is clearly inferable for the other magistrates as well. It was hardly possible to strike a more severe blow at the prerogatives of the popular courts. It was this right to call the magistrates to an accounting for their conduct in office that gave the dicasteries the whip hand in Athenian government. At some point between 106/5 and 101/0 B.C. they lost it to the Council. Obviously they had not regained it in 91–88 B.C. At that time Athenion, as reported by Posidonios (*Athen.*, V, 213d) speaks of the dicasteries as "silent" (ἄφωνα).

After capturing Athens in 86 B.C. Sulla "gave to the Athenians substantially [1] the same laws that had been previously established for them by the Romans" (νόμους ἔθηκεν ἅπασιν ἀγχοῦ τῶν πρόσθεν αὐτοῖς ὑπὸ Ῥωμαίων ὁρισθέντων; Appian, *Mith.*, 39; cf. *Strabo*, IX, 1, 20, 398). It is clear from IG^2 II 1039 (81/0? B.C.) that an essential provision of the Sullan constitution was the transfer to the Council of the legislative powers of the Ecclesia (see Kirchner's note). This was certainly not a feature of the Athenian laws for the period following 146 B.C. As late as the year 95/4 B.C. (IG^2 II 1029) the Ecclesia was competent for precisely the matters (grants of honors to ephebes and their officers) which after 86 B.C. belonged to the sole competence of the Council. Consequently, some of "the laws previously established by the Romans" were enacted after 95/4 B.C. It cannot be doubtful when the deposition of the Ecclesia took

[1] The limitation may have reference to the renewal of the ancient prohibition against repeated tenure of the archonships.

place. It occurred after 95/4 and prior to the return of Athenion from Pontos. Then, not only were "the dicasteries voiceless," but the theatre was "deserted by the Assembly" (ἀνεκκλησίαστον), and the Pnyx, "once consecrated to sacred uses by divine oracles, was taken away from the people" (πύκνα ἀφῃρημένην τοῦ δήμου; Posid., *loc. cit.*). The elimination of the Ecclesia indubitably was an accompaniment of the "dictatorship" of Medeios, who held the archonship for three years in succession (91/0–89/8 B.C.). This period is designated *anarchia* in the speech composed by Posidonios for Athenion, and had the "democrats" constructed the list of archons which has reached us (*IG* II 1713; Ditt.; *Syll.*³, 733), it would have been in these years, and not in 88/7 B.C., that the entry "*Anarchia*" would have appeared. A conceivable alternative for this radical departure is the "dictatorship" of Argeios, who held the archonship irregularly for a second year in 97/6 B.C., but this is excluded by *IG*² II 1029 which shows the Ecclesia still functioning as usual in 95/4 B.C.

Dinsmoor (p. 246) is unquestionably right in thinking that, not Argeios alone, but the other magistrates as well, including the priests, were continued in office irregularly in 97/6 B.C.[1] It is, I think, probable that under Medeios (91/0–89/8 B.C.) a similar situation existed. At any rate Dinsmoor's list of priests (p. 245)

[1] A further irregularity is to be noted in 98/7 B.C. (*IG*² II 2336, ll. 179 ff.). Medeios of the Piraeus held two Delian offices simultaneously, the governor-generalship and the presidency of the public bank. He was also *agonothetes* of the Panathenaia and the Delia. That this was irregular is shown by the fact that under Athenion his name was excised, to be recut after March, 86 B.C. (Wilhelm, *Attische Urkunden*, III, 1925, p. 59). In 97/6 B.C. Sarapion of Melite monopolized the *agonothesiae*.

contains no names for these years.² Obviously religious ceremonies were suspended. Posidonios makes Athenion declare in 89/8 B.C. "our holy places are kept locked against us, our gymnasia are in squalid decay, - - the sacred voice of Iacchus is sealed in silence and the august temple of the Two Divinities (Demeter and Kore) is closed." He is corroborated by IG^2 II 1338 (84/3? B.C.), where also the construction of an altar and temenos, destroyed "in the general calamity" (διὰ τὴν κοινὴν περίστασιν), is alluded to.

Clearly something out of the usual happened in or before 91 B.C. to enable Medeios to become archon in 91/0. Since he had held this office in 101/0 B.C., and iteration of office was still prohibited by law, as the archon list shows, he must have overridden the constitution in 91 B.C. Athens was obviously going through a succession of crises at this time: the transfer of the control of the magistrates from the dicasteries to the Council in ca. 103 B.C.; the usurpation of Argeios in 97/6; the reëlection of Medeios to the archonship in 91/0 and his tenure of it till the popular uprising in favor of Mithradates in 89/8. The suppression of the Assembly belongs to the last of these crises. From Posidonios we learn that on the return of Athenion from Mithradates in 89/8 B.C. the Ecclesia gathered in the Kerameikos "self-summoned" (αὐτόκλητος). We may infer that the Council was unable or unwilling to convene it.

The Romans took a hand in the course of this development. At the time of Athenion's arrival, as we learn

---

[1] It seems to me likely that Philokrates, son of Philokrates, who is noted as having been priest of Sarapis twice (δίς), held the office at this time (Roussel, *Cultes égyptiens à Délos*, pp. 190 f.; *Délos*, p. 349, n. 1; Dinsmoor, p. 238, n. 1).

again from Posidonios, the Roman Senate had the question under consideration as to how Athens was to be governed. "Then," he relates, "Athenion rubbed his forehead and said: 'What, now, am I to advise you? Tolerate no more the anarchical state of things which the Roman Senate has caused to be extended until such time as it shall decide what form of government we are to have.'" In a case of this sort the first resort was naturally to the court of the Roman praetor in Macedon who had had general oversight of Greek affairs since 146 B.C. If it were not for the statement of Appian quoted above (p. 150) we should be inclined to believe that the suppression of the *demos* was the result of a local *coup d'état*. In the light of his report we may conclude that it was countenanced if not prompted by the Macedonian governor, from whose judgment the Athenians had appealed to the Senate, which, in turn, had procrastinated, to say the least. And we shall not, I believe, err when we detect the will, if not the hand, of Rome behind the whole succession of crises, the tendency and goal of which were the suppression of popular liberties in the interest of a more oligarchical form of government. Such revolutionary changes in the government of Athens cannot have been effected without appeals to Rome by their opponents, if not by their proponents. Eventually it was rather the Council of the Areopagus than the Council of the Six Hundred which benefited; but provisionally the smaller body to be exalted was the latter, now doubtless much more timocratic in character than in the old days. The prerogatives of the Areopagus seem to have advanced *pari passu* with those of its more democratic partner;

but this advance can be connected with a change in its personnel, and does not require, to be intelligible, a remodelling of the "laws." After 86 B.C. it consciously imitated the procedure of the Roman Senate and aspired to its powers as the supreme advisory body.

The upshot of this inquiry into the forms of Athenian government is that it was in the fifteen years prior to the outbreak in 89/8 B.C. that the laws, restored by Sulla, were imposed upon their "allies" by the Romans, and not in 146 B.C. In regard to the epoch following the reduction of the Achaean League I can only repeat what I have already written (*Klio*, 1904, p. 16; Dinsmoor, p. 234), that "there is not the slightest evidence that the Romans altered the constitution of Athens" in or immediately after 146 B.C.[1] Dinsmoor (pp. 236 ff.) has established 145 B.C. as the epochal year of the Achaean Era, and has made plausible the idea that this has significance in the history of the Athenian calendar (p. 415); but we have as yet no record of the use of this Era by the Athenians. The beginning in 145 B.C. of the Great Archon-list (IG^2 II 1713), which was inscribed on stone in 44 A.D. (Dinsmoor, pp. 282 ff.), is to be connected, not with the introduction of this Era (on its replacement by the Actian Era in 32/1 B.C. this Era was discontinued; hence in 44 A.D. its very existence was doubtless forgotten, if not everywhere, certainly outside the areas of its use), but with the starting in that year of a new record of archons (the first after 146 B.C.) coincident with the inauguration of a

---

[1] The chief change, apart from details, I have to make in the account given in *Hellenistic Athens* of developments in Athens in the epoch prior to 89/8 B.C. is to recognize a series of crises, not one crisis alone in *ca.* 103 B.C.

new secretary-cycle (cf. Dinsmoor, p. 237). Athens was on the side of Rome during the Achaean War and was in no way involved politically in its consequences. It had, of course, to submit to the general rule that Greek affairs should be carried in the first instance to the court of the praetor established in 148 B.C. in Macedon, as is shown notably by the history of the Athenian guild of Dionysiac artists (*Hell. Ath.*, pp. 370 f.). But we have no reason to suppose that the Romans interfered with the domestic institutions of Athens in 146/5 B.C. These continued after as before, without perceptible change. After all, it was in her rôle as arbitrator of international differences that Rome became concerned in the affairs of the artists.

The point of this argument is that there is no reason why 146/5 B.C. should be thought appropriate for changes in Athenian Tribal Cycles.

XIV. Tribal Cycles of Athenian Priests at Delos

Dinsmoor has brought into relief the significance of 110/09 B.C. in the history of the priestly cycles: the extant list of priests of Sarapis ends in that year with the completion of a Tribal Cycle — another instance of the use of cycles as the limits of Athenian records; and in 109/8 B.C. a new cycle begins, not with the first *phyle*, Erechtheis, but with the eleventh, Antiochis. From that point it was maintained without a break to 95/4 B.C., and probably to what the democrats called the anarchy of 91/0. The list of priests of Asklepios (now IG^2 II 1944) published by Miss Guarducci (*Riv. di Fil.*, 1927, pp. 505 ff.) and combined by Roussel (*BCH*, 1928, pp. 1 ff.) with IG^1 II 958, begins with a priest from

TABLE VI
(Delian Priestly Cycles)

Year	Sarapis	No. of Phyle	Great Gods	No. of Phyle	Artemis	No. of Phyle	Zeus Kynthios	No. of Phyle
166/5		4		5				1
165/4	Kydantidai?	V		6				2
164/3		6		7				3
163/2		7		8				4
162/1		8		9				5
161/0	Anakaia?	IX	Marathon?	X				6
160/9	Trikorynthos?	X		11				7
159/8		11	Sunion?	XII				8
158/7		12		1				9
157/0	Hamaxanteia	IX	Pergase	I	Melite	VIII	Semachidai	V or XI
156/5								
155/4	Lamptrai?	I						
154/3								
153/2					Perithoidai?	VII		
152/1								
151/0								
150/9								
149/8								

148/7			
147/6			
146/5			
145/4		1	10
144/3		2	11
143/2		3	12
142/1		4	1
141/0		5	2
140/9		6	3
139/8		7	4
138/7		8	5
137/6	Eleusis & ——	IX	6
136/5	Trikorynthos	X	7
135/4	Anaphlystos	XI	8
134/3	Sunion	XII	9
133/2	Lamptrai	I	10
132/1	Philaidai	II	11
131/0	Paiania	III	12
130/9	Leukonoe	IV	1
129/8	Phlya	V	2
128/7	Kerameikos	VI	3
127/6	Acharnai	VII	4

[157]

TABLE VI (*Continued*)

Year	Sarapis	No. of Phyle	Great Gods	No. of Phyle	Artemis	No. of Phyle	Zeus Kynthios	No. of Phyle
126/5	Melite	VIII	Koile	IX				5
125/4		9		10				6
124/3	Marathon	X		11				7
123/2	Alopeke	XI		12				8
122/1	Tyrmeidai	XII		1				9
121/0	Pergase	I		2				10
120/9	Myrrhinoutta & Otryne	II	Myrrhinus	III				11
119/8	Paiania	III		4			Sunion	XII
118/7	Kolone	IV		5				1
117/6	Phlya	V		6				2
116/5	Thorikos & Sphettos	VI		7				3
115/4	Acharnai	VII		8				4
114/3	Melite	VIII	Piraeus	IX				5
113/2	Piraeus & Eroiadai	IX		10				6
112/1	Rhamnus	X		11				7
111/0	Anaphlystos	XI		12			Kikynna?	VIII
110/9	Oinoe	XII		1				9

Year	Sarapis	No. of Phyle	Anios	No. of Phyle	Artemis	No. of Phyle	Zeus Kynthois	No. of Phyle
109/8		11		10		8		7
108/7		12		11		9		8
107/6	Kephisia	I		12		10		9
106/5	Philaidai	II		1		11		10
105/4	Kydathenaion	III		2		12	Pallene?	XI
104/3	Kropidai	IV		3		1		12
103/2	Phlya	V	Skambonidai	IV	Ankyle	II	Kephisia	I
102/1		6		5	Kydathenaion	III		2
101/0	Acharnai	VII	Kerameikos	VI	Kolone	IV	Halimus	3
100/9	Melite	VIII		7		5	Aigilia	IV
99/8		9		8		6		V
98/7	Marathon	X		9		7		6
97/6								
96/5	Eitea	XI		10	Melite	VIII	Acharnai	VII
95/4		12						
94/3	Lamptrai	I						
93/2	Ionidai	II						
92/1	Kydathenaion	III						

A. Four other priests of Sarapis of the period 166/5–158/7 B.C. (Eirenaios, Ammonios, Sarapion, and Leon) are listed by Roussel (*Cultes égyptiens à Délos*, Table following p. 272).

B. For Athenogenes, son of Tisarchos, of Halimus (omitted by Dinsmoor), who was priest of Zeus Kynthios in 100/99 B.C., see Roussel, *Délos*, p. 494; *Explor. arch. de Délos*, XI, p. 126.

Erechtheis (I), not, as the cycle thitherto followed demanded, with a priest from Aiantis (X). There is no difficulty in assuming that the cycle thus reinaugurated, was also continued to 91/0 B.C.; and, as we have known for some time (*Priests of Asklepios*, pp. 144 f.), it was resumed after the official anarchy of 88/7 B.C., again, as in 109/8 B.C., with Erechtheis (I). And cycles in official order, traceable back to 109 B.C., existed down to the dissolution of democracy in Athens in the case of the priesthoods of Zeus Kynthios, Artemis, and Anios (Dinsmoor, pp. 245 f.; cf. Table VI).

The reallocation of priesthoods to *phylae* in 109 B.C. was not associated, apparently, with a political upheaval. Neither the Athenian nor the Delian records hint at any political changes at this time. The secretary-cycle continues undisturbed. The *antigrapheus*? for 109/8 B.C. (IG^2 II 1014), Stratios of Phegaia (III or II), follows the *antigrapheus* for 145/4 B.C. (IG^2 II 967), Demokrates of Kydathenaion (III), in unbroken cyclic relation.[1] So

[1] It may be noted in this connection that the fourth-century officials entitled ἐπὶ τὰ ψηφίσματα succeeded one another in the official order in the only instances in which we have their names: in 343/2 B.C. Demophilos of Agryle from Erechtheis (IG^2 II 223) and in 335/4 Kriton of Marathon from Aiantis (IG^2 II, 1700). In 335/4, as it happens, the prytany-secretary, the ἐπὶ τὰ ψηφίσματα, and the *antigrapheus* came from the eighth, ninth, and tenth *phylae*. I now believe that Brillant (*Les secrétaires athéniens*, pp. 97 ff.) is right in making the ἐπὶ τὰ ψηφίσματα, and hence Aristotle's secretary ἐπὶ τοὺς νόμους (*Ath. Pol.*, 54, 4), with whom he is to be identified, a subordinate colleague of the prytany-secretary, serving like his superior for a year. The *antigrapheus* was doubtless another. I cannot agree with Kirchner (*Ath. Mitt.*, 1904, pp. 245 ff.; IG^2 II iv, p. 46) and Dinsmoor (p. 353) that the ἐπὶ τὰ ψηφίσματα is identical with the secretary of the Council found with diminishing frequency in the publication-formula of decrees between 363 and 318/7 B.C. interchangeably with the prytany-secretary (for statistics see Dinsmoor, p. 352, n. 2). If, as it now appears, he rotated κατὰ φυλάς in the official order, he was an annual officer: the secretary of the Council, had he

far as we can see, the reallocation of 109 B.C. was confined to the priestly offices.[1] It probably signifies an

---

existed at all after 366 B.C., should have changed with the prytany. Certainly the argument for his existence which makes him the continuator of the secretary of the Council before 366 B.C. and identical with the secretary of 321/0–319/8 B.C. (Dinsmoor, p. 353) lacks all cogency if he did not change with the prytany. If, on the other hand, he was an annual official, why is he called secretary of laws or secretary of decrees? In other words, I still think, with Brillant and Rehm (*Ber. Phil. Woch.*, 1916, pp. 299 f.), that γραμματεὺς τῆς βουλῆς, like γραμματεὺς τοῦ δήμου between 307/6 and 200 B.C., was simply a variant title for γραμματεὺς κατὰ πρυτανείαν.

Besides the two *antigrapheis* mentioned in the text, we know the name and date of only one other of these checking- or copying-clerks: Pistoklees of Anaphlystos in 335/4 B.C. In 145/4–109/8 B.C. Antiochis, the *phyle* to which he belonged, followed that of the prytany-secretary by the same interval as in 335/4 B.C. I suggest as a possibility to be kept in mind that prytany-secretary, secretary of laws or decrees, and *antigrapheus* (ὁ γραμματεὺς ὁ κατὰ πρυτανείαν καὶ οἱ ἄλλοι γραμματεῖς οἱ ἐπὶ τοῖς δημοσίοις γράμμασιν, IG^2 II 120, ll. 15 ff.), chosen as a block from consecutive *phylae*, followed the same scheme of Tribal Cycles throughout. On this assumption IG^2 II 1740 (with an *antigrapheus* Aristion? of Pallene, X) would belong in 345/4 B.C., or a decade or two earlier or later.

Furthermore, if the observation regarding the secretary of decrees is correct, this official is not to be identified with the secretary of the Council and *demos*, as Kirchner (*loc. cit.*, p. 246) and Schulthess (*PW*, VII, p. 1729) claim; for in 334/3 B.C. (IG^2 II 1750) the latter (Pronapes of Prospalta) came from Akamantis (V), whereas the former should have come from Aigeis (II). If the secretary of the Council and *demos* had his own Tribal Cycle, IG^2 II 1740 (with . . . . leides of Oion, IV or VIII holding this secretaryship) could still belong in 345/4 B.C. or its alternates. But in that case the secretary of the *demos* of IG^2 II 1700 (335/4 B.C.) would have to be a different secretary, which is highly improbable. Since, however, the secretary of the Council and *demos*, when identified with the third of Aristotles' secretaries, the one who read documents to the Council and *demos*, was chosen, not by sortition, but by show of hands, we should not expect him to have rotated by *phylae*. Hitherto we have found no annual office to which *cheirotonia* applied rotating κατὰ φυλάς.

[1] The restoration περὶ ἱερῶν in the prescript of IG^2 II 1014 (109/8 B.C.) is given only *exempli gratia* by Wilhelm (*Beiträge*, p. 283), but may well be right. *Hiera*, however, means, doubtless, "religious business," not "shrines."

attempt to effect a more equitable distribution of the corps of Athenian and Delian priests among the *phylae*. It was timed to coincide with the simultaneous termination of various Tribal Cycles (the secretary-cycle, the priestly cycles of Sarapis and Asklepios) and of the Metonic Cycle; and it may have been occasioned by the extension to yet more priesthoods of rotation in the official order.

Rotation in the official order was not established for all the priesthoods in 109 B.C. The priest of Dionysos at Delos for 101/0 B.C. came from Halai? (II or VIII) and in 98/7 from Athmonon (XII); the four priests of the Delian Apollo whose demes and dates (Pambotadai, 103/2; Epikephisia, 101/0; Anaphlystos, 100/99; Philaidai, 99/8 B.C.) are known came from *phylae* I, VII, XI, and II respectively; and the three priests of Roma at Delos who are similarly defined (Sunion, 103/2; Aixone, 101/0; Halai, 96/5 B.C.) came from *phylae* XII, VIII, and II (or VIII). No cyclic relation existed in any of these three cases. With the exception of the last priest of Roma all these priests belong in the Tribal Cycle running from 109/8 to 98/6 B C. It is significant, therefore, that no *phyle* held the same priesthood twice in the period. The inference is, accordingly, permissible that these priesthoods rotated among the *phylae*, not indeed in the official order, but in an allotted order. This conclusion may be drawn with almost complete certainty in the case of the priesthood of Hagne Aphrodite at Delos. So far as they are determinable the priests of this goddess are listed in Table VII,

The definition of cycles is conjectural. I have assumed that 109 B.C., here as elsewhere, was the point of divi-

TABLE VII

Year	Priest	His deme	No. of Phyle	Year	Priest	His deme	No. of Phyle
121/0				109/8			
120/9				108/7	Nikostratos	Lamptrai	I
119/8				107/6	Aischrion	Melite	VIII
118/7	Menodoros?*	Myrrhinoutta	II	106/5	Zoilos	Phlya	V
117/6				105/4	Philoxenos	Sunion	XII
116/5	Gaios?	Acharnai	VII	104/3			
115/4				103/2	Diophantos	Marathon	X
114/3				102/1	Thea-		
113/2	Theodotos?	Sunion	XII	101/0	Aristonus	Sphettos	VI
112/1	Theodoros	Aithalidai	IV	100/9			
111/0				99/8			
110/9	Demonikos	Anaphlystos	XI	98/7	Theobios?†	Acharnai	VII
				97/6	Theobios	Acharnai	VII

* Priests whose names are followed by an interrogation point are only approximately dated.
† Theobios is assumed to have served during both archonships of Argeios (Dinsmoor, p. 245). In 96/5 B.C. he was priest of Zeus Kynthios. In some year between 96/5 and 89/8 B.C., i.e., in the next cycle, Seleukos of Acharnai (VII) was priest.

sion; and this assumption is commended by the issue, that on their creation the priests of Aphrodite adopted the cycle of the priests of Sarapis. The precise year of the first establishment of an Athenian priesthood of the Delian Aphrodite is indeterminate: it lies between 128 (123?) and 118 B.C. (Roussel, *Délos*, pp. 256 ff.), and 121 B.C., the beginning of the assumed cycle, is not improbable. The point is that the facts tabulated are inexplicable without the hypothesis that the office rotated among all the *phylae* by allotment: there must surely have been double representation of some one *phyle* in the period following 109 B.C. if that had been possible. It is worth noting by way of contrast that where this possibility existed double representation at short intervals was frequent. Thus Antiochis had the governor-generalship of Delos five times and Oineis and Hippothontis each at least three times between 128/7 and 104/3 B.C., while between 137/6 and 112/1 B.C. Akamantis and Aiantis had the gymnasiarchy at Delos five times each. Similarly, between 451/0 and 440/39 B.C. Leontis held the clerkship of the Hellenotamiae four times.

We are, accordingly, justified in looking elsewhere for cycles of allotted priests; and the period which interests us especially is the one running from 157/6 to 146/5 B.C. during which, as we have seen, the secretaryship was distributed among the *phylae* by sortition. Roussel (*Délos*, pp. 349 f.) has observed that two priests of Sarapis who held office prior to the end of the archonship of Anthesterios, namely, Philokrates of Hamaxanteia and Ktesippos of Anakaia (cf. Roussel, *Cultes égyptiens a Délos*, p. 224, n. 6), came from the same *phyle* (Hippothontis) and infers a temporary absence of rotation of the office among the *phylae* (cf. Dinsmoor, p. 239, n. 2). If, however, the rotation existed, but the order of the *phylae* was determined by lot, two priests from Hippothontis would be possible, but only if the period of allotment was limited to the cycle 157/6–146/5 B.C. If rotation in the official order began in 166/5 B.C. (when the priesthood was first inaugurated) with Leontis (IV), as it should if retrojected from 137/6 B.C.,[1] we can avoid a period of tribal irregularity altogether, but only when Anthesterios is dated as late as 157/6 B.C. The outside limits for Anthesterios are 158/7 and 156/5 B.C. (Dinsmoor, p. 262, with corrections necessitated by dating Aristolas in 161/0 B.C.). For dating him in the precise year in which Philokrates of Hamaxanteia was priest, there is one favoring consideration and another which has been taken hitherto to be prohibitive. Offerings made to Sarapis "in the

[1] The "great" list of priests of Sarapis (*BCH*, 1893, pp. 146 f.; *Athenian Secretaries*, pp. 46 ff.; Roussel, *Cultes égyptiens a Délos*, pp. 122 f., cf. *Délos*, p. 348, n. 3; Dinsmoor, pp. 228 f.) begins as follows:

[Τ]ιμ-
Δημόσ[ιος]
Δημόσιο[s]
(137/6 B.C.) Φανόβιος Ἐλευσίνιο[s καί]
Δημήτριος

It is incredible that an Athenian was called Demosios. Roussel (*Délos*, p. 349, n. 2; *Cultes égyptiens a Délos*, p. 124) suggests that for two years a *demosios* replaced the priest. This would, of course, dislocate the official order. At the least it would push the cycle back two places. It seems to me more likely that in 138/7 B.C. an inventory of the Sarapieion was made in which, in consonance with Athenian practice (*IG*² II 839, 840, 1539), *demosioi* participated. The fact that the cycle, when retrojected from 137/6 B.C., places Erechtheis precisely in 145/4 B.C. indicates, I think, that the two *demosioi* did not replace priests.

priesthood of Philokrates" are recorded under the heading "these also we took over in addition" (καὶ τάδε προσπαρελάβομεν) in the inventory of Anthesterios' year. The natural inference is that they were made in Anthesterios' year (Roussel, *Délos*, p. 349, n. 1), and, if so, Philokrates was also priest in that year. But, as Roussel remarks, their entry under the same heading in the inventory of the following year (that of Kallistratos; cf. *Cultes égyptiens a Délos*, p. 224, l. 70) permits us to believe that the rubric was *tralaticia* and that they were received earlier than the year of Anthesterios (cf. Dinsmoor, p. 238). Roussel suggests for the priesthood of Philokrates the year immediately preceding the archonship of Anthesterios. The consideration held to be repugnant to dating the priest Philokrates and the archon Anthesterios in the same year is that the commissioners of the Sacred Fund are apparently different in the years of the two officials. This is a point, however, which requires further investigation.

In Metageitnion of Anthesterios' year the commissioners of the Sacred Fund were Diophantos of Hermos and Theodoros of Marathon. These same men appear as tenants of the same charge in the month of Metageitnion in the archonship of Kallistratos (*BCH*, 1910, p. 183, n. 2), whereas in the month of Skirophorion in the archonship of Kallistratos this charge was held by Kallias of Gargettos and Ephialtes of Sybridai (Roussel, *Délos*, pp. 132, n. 2; 140, n. 1; 141; 358; Dinsmoor, p. 506). It follows that at this time the term of office of the commissioners began in the course of the month Metageitnion. Accordingly, when we date the archonship of Anthesterios in 157/6 B.C. (156/5 is the only alternative), the commissioners in office during its first month (Hekatombaion) and part of its second were those of the Delian financial year 158/7 B.C.[1] At the moment at which Philokrates "became" priest of Sarapis [2] the commissioners were —, son of -ippos, of

[1] Notoriously the year of the *kosmetes* in Athens and his colleagues on the ephebe staff began at this time with Boedromion, two months later than that of the other officials.

[2] We learn this from the Delian document published in *BCH*, 1908, p. 438, no. 64 (Pl. iv), cf. Roussel, *Délos*, p. 132, n. 4, the preamble of which may be restored, *exempli gratia*, as follows:

['Αγαθεῖ τύχει· ἐπὶ 'Ανθεστηρίου]
[ἄρχοντος, ἐπιμελήτου δὲ τῆς]
[νήσου — τ]οῦ 'Απο[λλο-   ]
[—   ] καὶ ἐπὶ τὴν [φυλακὴν]
[τῶν ἱερῶν χρη]μάτων —   ]
[— τοῦ -]ίππου 'Ερικ[έως καὶ]
[—   ] τοῦ Καλλικλ[έους]
[Προσπ]α[λ]τίου.
            [Ο]ἵδε ἐγέν[οντο ἱερεῖς]

Apollo?,	-s of Oion	(IV or XII)
Hestia and Roma,	-goras of Kropidai	(IV)
Zeus Kynthios,	Mikion of Semachidai	(V or XI)
Zeus Soter,	Ephoros of Ptelea	(VII)
Artemis,	Athenagoras of Melite	(VIII)
Great Gods,	Seleukos of Pergase	(I)
Dionysos,	Eumenes of Oinoe	(V or XII)
Asklepios,	Echos of Sunion	(XII)
Sarapis,	Philokrates of Hamaxanteia	(IX)
Anios,	Noumenios of Phyle	(VII)
Hierokeryx,	Dionysios of Lamptrai	(I)
Mantis,	Olympiodoros of Pallene	(XI)
Auletes,	Perigenes of Eupyridai	(IV)
Kleiduchos,	Nymphodoros of Marathon	(XI)

Since nothing further seems to have been written on the stone, the tablet can be taken to be simply a record of the priests made at the time of their election. It may have some significance that this list was set up at the beginning of the Tribal Cycle during which allotment supplanted the official order of the *phylae*.

Erikeia and —, son of Kallikles, of Prospalta. Since our evidence for the existence of a Delian year overlapping the Attic year concerns the commissioners alone (Roussel, *Délos*, p. 140, n. 1), there is no reason for supposing that the priestly year did not coincide with that of the Attic archon. Hence we can date —, son of -ippos, of Erikeia and —, son of Kallikles, of Prospalta in 158/7 B.C. and Anthesterios and Philokrates in 157/6. Roussel (*Délos*, p. 359) and Dinsmoor (p. 238) are, therefore, unjustified in holding that this is impossible.

This, however, involves placing the priest of the Great Gods, Seleukos of Pergase (I), in 157/6 B.C. also, since he and Philokrates were colleagues. That is not where his *phyle* belongs when the priestly cycle of the Great Gods which existed in 128/7, 126/5, and 120/19 B.C. is retrojected: it belongs rather in 158/7, and it is by following this lead that Roussel and Dinsmoor date both Seleukos and Philokrates in 158/7. Seleukos can belong in 157/6 B.C. only when we assume that in the case of this priesthood, as in that of the priesthood of Sarapis and the prytany-secretariat, there was a cycle of allotted *phylae* between 157/6 and 146/5 B.C. This, however, is precisely what we should expect. In all three cases the cycles begun in 166/5 B.C. were (we may conjecture) resumed with the official order in 145/4 B.C. when the cycle of allotted order was completed.

We are not able to prove that the priesthood of Zeus Kynthios rotated according to the official order between 145/4 B.C. and 110/09, but since such rotation is demonstrable after 109 B.C., it probably existed prior thereto; and the facts in our possession are reconcilable with this hypothesis. The priest for 119/8 B.C. (*BCH*, 1908, p. 429; Roussel, *Délos*, p. 226) was Lykophron of Sunion, of the *phyle* Attalis (XII). The priest Charmikos of Kikynna (VIII or VI), mentioned in connection with the archon Paramonos (*Explor. arch. de Délos*, XI, p. 96), probably belongs either in his year (113/2 B.C.) or in 111/0, thus establishing a cyclic relationship.[1] If this is correct, we have again to assume a cycle of allotted rotation in 157/6–146/5 B.C., since the priest of Zeus Kynthios in 157/6, Mikion of Semachidai, came from the Vth or XIth *phyle*, and not from the Xth. If, however, the alternate year, 156/5 B.C., were assigned to Anthesterios, this conclusion would be invalidated; but this the dating of Aristaichmos in 154/3 (Dinsmoor, pp. 263 ff.) prevents. For the two other priesthoods which observed the official order between 109/8 and 91 B.C., those of Anios and Artemis, we lack all information as to the tribal relations of priests between 145/4 and 110/09 B.C. Hence we can neither affirm nor deny that they used the period of allotted order in 157/6–146/5 B.C. The priestly cycles of Artemis prior to 109/8 B.C. are, accordingly, left blank in Table VI.[2]

The chances are, I think, that the priesthoods which followed an allotted order of *phylae* between 109/8 and

[1] We do not know that — of Marathon (X) was *priest* of Zeus Kynthios (*Explor. arch. de Délos*, XI, p. 117). In any event he cannot have been priest in the year of the Jason who held the archonship in 109/8 B.C. Nor, on the cycle established in Table VI, can he have been *priest* in 125/4.

[2] Roussel (*Délos*, p. 219, n. 7) identifies the Pylades of Perithoidai who held some Delian priesthood in the archonship of Phaidrias (153/2–149/8 B.C.) with the Pylades of Perithoidai who held the priesthood of Artemis in this general period (*ibid.*, p. 430, no. 57). If this is so, the priests of Artemis did not succeed one another in the fixed order of the *phylae* between 157/6 and 146/5 B.C.

91 B.C., those of Apollo, Roma, and Dionysos, observed cycles of allotted order throughout. Since Eumenes of Oinoe (V or XII) was priest of Dionysos in 157/6 and Eubulos of Marathon (X) in the archonship of Aristaichmos (154/3 B.C.), the official order was certainly not followed by this priesthood between 157/6 and 146/5 B.C.

On the conclusions thus far reached, those concerning 166/5 B.C. being highly problematical, priesthoods known to have observed the official order at some time were distributed in specific years among the *phylae* as follows:

TABLE VIII

Priesthood	166/5	157/6	145/4	109/8
Asklepios (Athenian)	12	..	10	1
Sarapis (Delian)	4	9	1	11
Great Gods "	5	1	2	..
Artemis "	..	8	..	8
Anios "	..	7	..	10
Zeus Kynthios "	1	5 or 11	10	7
Asklepios "	..	12	..	12?

In 145/4 B.C. the Athenian priest of Asklepios and the Delian priest of Zeus Kynthios were taken from the same *phyle*. The Delian priests in the group were invariably taken from different *phylae*. Can this be fortuitous? If we take into consideration the entire corps of Delian priests we encounter duplication of *phylae*: in 157/6 B.C., for example, either the IVth or the XIIth *phyle* had two priests, and in the archonship of Phaidrias (153/2? B.C.), though one priest is missing in our extant list (*BCH*, 1907, pp. 425 ff.), the

Ist *phyle* had three priests, the other six being from different *phylae*. At the time when all the priesthoods were distributed κατὰ φυλάς by lot (157/6–146/5 B.C.) such duplication was bound to occur if it was not systematically prevented, as in the case of the three senior archons (*above*, p. 53), or if the total number of priesthoods exceeded 12, — or 24, — as would be the case when the Delian and Athenian priesthoods were combined for allotment in one group. It would also be unavoidable in the case of the Delian priesthoods alone when some of them rotated by allotment and others by the fixed sequence. Hence I have limited the tabulation to the Delian priesthoods of the latter category. In their case annual distribution among the *phylae* was obviously prearranged. Nor do I believe that such distribution in 157/6 B.C. was fortuitous. Since it was the first year of rotation by allotment it seems likely that care was taken, by some such means as those used in the case of the senior archons, to prevent a single *phyle* from holding two of these priesthoods. Subsequently, as in 153/2? B.C., they may not have been so careful. In other words, we shall have to recognize that normally the Athenian-Delian priesthoods were distributed, to a certain extent at least, both horizontally, i.e., annually, κατὰ φυλάς, and vertically in tribal cycles. I take it that the reallocation of 109 B.C. was an effort to perfect yet further this system.

XV. The Change in the Priestly Cycle of Asklepios in 157 B.C.

The problem still faces us: What happened to the priestly cycle of the Athenian priests of Asklepios between 165/4 and 138/7 B.C. (*above*, pp. 139 f.)? That some dislocation occurred between these points is clear from the relation of this set of cycles to that of the secretaries: in 165/4 this was V:I, in 138/7, VIII:V (that is, V:II). Dinsmoor (p. 250) has shown that the relation VIII:V can have existed in the year 114/3 B.C.; but this is dependent upon the dating of the archon Pleistainos in that year, which, though it is probably correct, cannot be proved. There is apparently no escape (on my scheme of secretary-cycles) from the omission of one *phyle* in the priestly cycle of Asklepios between 165/4 and 138/7 B.C. How can we explain this omission?

We have no help from the records. Our knowledge of Athenian history at this time does not descend to such details. Certain possibilities may be mentioned. We might suppose that rotation in the official order was carried forward from 165/4 B.C. through the period 157/6–146/5 B.C. during which the prytany-secretaries and the Delian priests were assigned to the *phylae* by allotment. In 142/1 B.C. we should reach the close of a cycle. It happens that in 141/0 B.C. there were two gymnasiarchs at Delos, one from Leontis chosen by the *epimeletes* and the youths undergoing gymnasiastic training, the other from Aigeis chosen by the *demos*. In the course of this year Athens supplanted a gymnasiarch locally elected by one of its own choice. We may leave it undecided whether the local election in 141/0 B.C. was an usurpation of a prerogative of the central government (Roussel, *Délos*, pp. 188 f.) or the continuation of earlier practice (Dinsmoor, p. 231, n. 2). The fact is certain that Athens intervened in the course of the year to appoint a new gymnasiarch. We know that

Adeimantos of Ikaria was *epimeletes* of the island in 141/0 B.C. (Roussel, *Délos*, pp. 102, 133 ff.), and that the commissioners of the Sacred Fund were Euthydemos of Athmonon and Euktemon of Melite (*ibid.*, p. 142). We have no evidence that these officials did not serve for the entire year. It is possible that this crisis in the gymnasiarchy is to be connected with the dissolution of the Delian cleruchy (*Klio*, 1907, pp. 234 ff.; Hatzfeld, *BCH*, 1912, pp. 190 ff.; Roussel, *Délos*, pp. 50 ff.). The last manifestation of its existence which has reached us dates from 144/3 B.C., the archonship of Metrophanes' successor (*Klio*, 1907, p. 236, n. 1; Roussel, *Délos*, pp. 55, 362). But since the earliest activity of the aggregate which took its place does not antedate 130 B.C. (Roussel, *Délos*, pp. 51, 55, n. 4), there is as yet no means of dating the change precisely.

The situation which gave Delos two gymnasiarchs in 141/0 B.C. was doubtless primarily local, but it involved the central government. There is no apparent reason why it should have affected the priesthood of Asklepios in Athens; but if we should assume that there were also two priests in this year, one from Erechtheis and another from Aigeis, we could correlate the system of cycles that existed in 165/4 B.C. with that which existed in 138/7. This, however, is an unlikely assumption: we should expect the two priests to come from the same *phyle*; and it is based on another unlikely assumption, that the official order was maintained between 157/6 and 146/5 B.C. Since, moreover, it postulates a priestly cycle of Asklepios beginning with Erechtheis, i.e., *phyle* I, contrary to third century practice, it needs only to be stated to be rejected.

A second possibility is that in the cycle of allotted *phylae* (157/6–146/5 B.C.) a *phyle* was omitted somewhere, perhaps at 146/5–145/4 B.C., to effect a more equable tribal distribution of priesthoods. It is imaginable, for example, that in 146/5 B.C. the lot gave the priesthood of Asklepios to Hippothontis (IX) and that the official order was continued in 145/4 B.C. with Aiantis; overlooking the fact that the cycle of allotted *phylae* had eleven priests instead of twelve, realizing the conceivable desirability that the cycle should begin in 145/4 B.C. with Aiantis rather than with Hippothontis. It is, however, a weighty objection to this hypothesis that some one *phyle* would have been discriminated against without sufficient reason. Had there been a general reallocation of priesthoods in 145 B.C. such as occurred in 109 B.C., the assumed omission of a *phyle*, or of *phylae*, would have been tolerable, since what a *phyle* lost in one series of cycles it might gain in another. But we have no evidence that a general reallocation of priesthoods occurred in 145 B.C.

The solution of the problem is really quite simple. We have another case of the "privilege" of Aiantis (*above*, pp. 78 ff.). As we have seen (*above*, p. 62), on the earlier resumption in 276/5 B.C. of rotation in the official order after a period of rotation in an allotted order, the priest of Asklepios with whom the new cycle began was taken from Aiantis. Precisely the same procedure was followed in 145/4 B.C. The omission of a *phyle* was an inevitable consequence of the decision to recognize the historical right of Aiantis to head this cycle. The priestly cycle of Asklepios which was incomplete was the tenth, counting 276/5–265/4 B.C. as the first (cf.

Table II), — the one which was due to end in 157/6 B.C. This was terminated before the last *phyle* (Hippothontis) had had its turn by the general substitution in 157 B.C. of allotment of *phylae* for rotation in their fixed order, the point of this innovation being determined, not by the state of the priestly cycle of Asklepios, but by the termination in 158/7 B.C. of the secretary-cycle. The privilege of Aiantis could not be affirmed in 145/4 B.C. except at the expense of Hippothontis which, having lost its turn in 157/6 B.C., could have regained it only if the claim of Aiantis to lead the cycle were ignored. The slighting of Hippothontis was probably viewed in 145 B.C. as an inevitable consequence of the action of the Athenians in 157 B.C.

In view of the mode in which the priestly cycle of Asklepios was resumed in 145/4 B.C. it may be questioned whether the Delian priestly cycles between 166/5 and 158/7 B.C. are correctly established in Table VI; but in their case the privilege of Aiantis, so far as we can see, had no analogue.[1] It has seemed wise, however, to query in Table VI the dates assigned to the Delian priests of this epoch. They are subject to alteration when any of the priests of Sarapis, the Great Gods, and Zeus Kynthios between 166/5 and 158/7 B.C. are dated definitely.

Each of the twelve *phylae* had the priesthood of Asklepios between 157/6 and 146/5 B.C., and each of them had it again in the period from 145/4 to 134/3 B.C., and in the following Tribal Cycles, 133/2–122/1 and

[1] The case of the priestly cycle of Sarapis, which started off in 145/4 B.C. with Erechtheis, is not analogous, since this priesthood followed the same cycle as the prytany-secretary.

121/0–110/09 B.C.[1] On the general reallocation of priesthoods in 109 B.C. Erechtheis, which, of course, was always an alternate to Aiantis as coryphaeus, began the new cycle in 109/8 B.C. Tribal representation was thus preserved unbroken between 356/5? and 91 B.C. except possibly in 321/0–308/7 B.C. and in 157 B.C.

Epilogue

I should like to believe that the Tribal Cycles arranged in Tables II and VI (*above*, pp. 22 ff., 156 ff,) are a definite acquisition, and that, to quote a friendly French critic of my earlier effort in this field, *le seul travail qui reste à faire aujourd'hui, c'est de compléter à l'aide des inscriptions qui pourront être découvertes ultérieurement les listes déjà établies*. But when I reflect that the *Athenian Archons* was hardly printed before a Magnesian inscription came to light (Kern, *Inschriften von Magnesia*, no. 16) upsetting in an important particular a system of secretary-cycles in which I had great confidence, and that within five years of the appearance of the *Priests of Asklepios* my rectified scheme of Tribal Cycles was damaged uncomfortably by the publication of the list of Delian gymnasiarchs (*BCH*, 1912, p. 395); and when I call to mind the paucity and ambiguity of the evidence (in large part circumstantial) on which much of the

[1] At this time all the Tribal Cycles we are considering, excepting that of the *archontes* (cf. *above*, p. 51, n. 4), began and ended at the same point. It is not an accident that the reallocation of 109 B.C. coincided precisely with the termination of a Metonic Cycle. The only other occasion on which the Metonic Cycle and the secretary-cycle began at the same point is 356 B.C., when the official order was first introduced (cf. Dinsmoor, p. 354; *Treasurers of Athena*, pp. 142 f.).

construction rests, I do not dare to hope that the Tribal Cycles of Athens in the Hellenistic Age are now established beyond the possibility of subsequent change. Yet Dinsmoor's new inscription has helped us safely across one bad place (289–7 B.C.) and his acumen has bridged another (103/2 B.C.). He has laid, I trust for good and all, the spectre of inflexible calendar cycles which Beloch had invoked. It gives me a certain measure of confidence in the results of my work that, with little or no effort on my part, the dates assigned by me to the archons harmonize completely with the flexible calendar with which Dinsmoor, by inductive methods, has replaced the theoretical constructions hitherto current (*non peccavi*). One by one historic facts which seemed to be recalcitrant, and at times actually were such, have ceased to be obstacles, and have become instead supports, of the Tribal Cycles now that their limits are more accurately defined. I am unaware of any historical data to which the present system does injustice. Out of the new materials added by me to the *dossier* I should like to pick as particularly reassuring (to me at least) the testimony of the groups of archon-names adduced at pages 83 ff. If it tells the story to others that it tells to me the Tribal Cycles *are* definitely established at crucial points, and subsequent rectifications can only concern details.

To me this study has been a fascinating puzzle. It has also given me a more concrete appreciation of certain aspects of Athenian democracy. As cycle after cycle has come to view, the intricate tribal design which underlay the routine administrative service of the Athenians has been more and more clearly revealed.

The mechanism devised by them for the proportionate division of offices was obviously worked out with a finesse and attention to detail comparable with the exactitude and igenuity employed by them in organizing for the same purpose their deliberative and judicial organs. "The characteristics of democracy," Aristotle tells us (*Pol.*, VIII (VI), 2, 5, p. 1317b), "are as follows: the election of officers by all out of all; and that all should rule over each, and each in his turn over all; that the appointment to all offices, or to all but those which require experience and skill, should be made by lot; that no property qualification should be required for offices, or only a very low one; that a man should not hold the same office twice, or not often, or in the case of few except military offices: that the tenure of all offices, or of as many as possible, should be brief." [1] It is illuminating to see how these principles, applied to annual offices held by individuals, were adhered to cycle after cycle and century after century, and to speculate on how they were, on occasions, annulled. The withdrawal of all candidates for the archonship in favor of the one whose name, or dignity, or patronage made his election desirable would save the system by circumventing it. We may conjecture that this happened in 261/0–255/4, 166–4, and 86/5 B.C. In the Hellenistic age the *phylae* were obviously more insistent on preserving their electoral rights and privileges than individuals.

[1] Translation by Jowett in Ross' *Works of Aristotle in English Translation*, Vol. X.

ADDENDA

The detailed reviews of Dinsmoor's *Archons of Athens* by Kirchner (*Gnomon*, 1932, pp. 449 ff.), Kahrstedt (*GGA*, 1932, pp. 305 ff.), and Roussel (*REA*, 1932, pp. 196 ff.) arrived after this monograph was in page-proof. Roussel reports (on the basis of an unpublished document) that the archon for 114/3 B.C. was -rates or -ratos. Hence Ple- (Pleistainos) and the priest of Asklepios, Leonides? of Phlya, do not belong in that year. He also reports the existence of a new document with the archon-name — με]τὰ Τιμαρχίδην. If the successor of Timarchides (136/5 B.C.) was Ergokles (Table II), another Ergokles was archon not long before him. It seems not improbable, therefore, that the archon for 144/3 B.C. was, after all, Ergokles (Hermias is purely hypothetical). I may add that Mikion can belong in 154/3–148/7 B.C. instead of in 132/1 B.C. We might then put Aristaichmos in 158/7, Nikomachos in 134/3, Xenon (a fixed point) in 133/2, Ergokles in 132/1, and Epikles in 131/0 B.C., thus leaving 135/4 B.C. for a Dionysios, as desiderated by Roussel. This would require us to treat the undeciphered passages in Mekler, *Acad. Phil. Index Herc.*, p. 106, col. 33 which follow δέκα [κ]αὶ τ[έτ]ταρα (l.12) and δέ[κα] (l.14) as explanatory additions such as Philodemos often inserts. We should then divide the life of Philon into three periods of 24, 14, and 10 years respectively.

Page 13 (cf. p. 89). From the traces of letters left in the erasure in line six of *BCH*, 1930, p. 269, Dow and Meritt conclude that the word excised is ['Ἀντιγόνο]υ, instead of [Δημητρίο]υ. If it was from Antigonus that Dikaiarchos and Apollonios received their appointment at Rhamnus, this objection to Dinsmoor's dating of Ekphantos in 239/8 B.C. falls to the ground.

Page 145, n. 1. On reflection Dinsmoor's reasons appear less decisive. The alternate initial date for the list of Delian gymnasiarchs, 167/6 B.C., would leave the Tribal Cycles unaltered. The archons Aristophon, Theaitetos, E-, Metrophanes, Epikrates, and Archon would simply be moved back a year. There is no difficulty in the assumptions that Erechtheis was the *phyle* to secure the secretariat last in the cycle of allotted order, and that the secretary for the year of E- came from Erechtheis.

BIBLIOGRAPHY

Since a full Bibliography appears in Dinsmoor, W. B., *The Archons of Athens in the Hellenistic Age*, Cambridge, Mass., 1931, pp. 515 ff., it will suffice to add the following titles:

Beloch, K. J.
"Μίθρης." *Riv. di Fil.*, 1926, pp. 331 ff.

Boesch, P.
Θεωρός, Berlin, 1908.

De Sanctis, G.
"Cronologia della prima guerra macedonica." *Storia dei Romani*, III 2, pp. 440 ff. Milano, Torino, Roma, 1917.

Ferguson, W. S.
The Treasurers of Athena, Cambridge, Mass., 1932.

Herzog, R.
"Griechische Königsbriefe." *Hermes*, 1930, pp. 470 ff.

Holleaux, M.
"Remarques sur les décrets des villes de Crète relatifs à l'ἀσυλία de Téos." *Klio*, 1913, pp. 137 ff.

Holleaux, M., et Robert, L.
"Nouvelles remarques sur l'édit d'Ériza." *BCH*, 1930, pp. 259 f.

Keil, B.
"Beiträge zur Geschichte des Areopags." *Ber. der Gesell. der Wissen. zu Leipzig*, LXXI 8, 1919, p. 27.

Kolbe, W.
"Die griechische Politik der ersten Ptolemaeer." *Hermes*, 1916, p. 545, n. 1.

Kougeas, S.
"Ὁ Δημητριακὸς πόλεμος καὶ αἱ Ἀθῆναι." Ἑλληνικά, III, pp. 281 ff.

Laqueur, R.
Epigraphische Untersuchungen zu den griechischen Volksbeschlüssen, pp. 32 ff. Leipzig, Berlin, 1927.

Levi, M. A.
"La cronologia degli strateghi Etolici degli anni 221–168 a.C." *Atti della Accad. di Torino*, LVII, 1921/2, pp. 179 ff.

Mathieu, G.
"Notes sur Athènes a la veille de la guerre lamiaque: III. La population de la Léontis au IVe siècle." *Rev. de Phil.*, 1929, pp. 179 ff.

Meyer, Ed.
"Die Schlacht von Pydna." *Sitz. der preuss. Akad.*, 1909, pp. 780 ff.

Nock, A. D.
"Σύνναος Θεός." *Harvard Studies in Class. Phil.*, XLI (1930), pp. 60 f.

Otto, W.
"Beiträge zur Seleukidengeschichte des 3. Jahrhunderts v. Chr." *Abh. der bayerischen Akad.*, XXXIV 1, 1928, pp. 46 ff.
"Zu den syrischen Kriegen der Ptolemäer." *Philologus*, 1931, pp. 416 ff.

Robert, L.
"Notes d'épigraphie hellénistique: XXXVI. Sur les Sôteria de Delphes; XXXVII. Sur les Nikephoria de Pergame." *BCH*, 1930, pp. 322 ff., 332 ff.

Roussel, P.
"Un nouveau document relatif a la guerre démétriaque." *BCH*, 1930, pp. 268 ff.

Segre, M.
"Olimpiodoro e il dominio macedonico sul Pireo." *Annuario del R. Liceo Dante Alighieri di Bressanone*, 1928/9 (reprint), pp. 1 ff.
"L'asilia di Smirne e le Soterie di Delfi." *Historia*, 1931, pp. 241 ff.
"Note epigrafiche: II. Διονύσια καὶ Δημητρίεια." *Il Mondo Classico*, 1932, pp. 288 ff.

Stählin, Fr.
"Die Phthiotis und der Friede zwischen Philippos V. und den Aetolern." *Philologus*, 1921, pp. 199 ff.
Das hellenische Thessalien, pp. 159 ff. Stuttgart, 1924.

STAVROPOULLOS, PH.
"Τιμητικὸν Ψήφισμα ἐκ Ραμνοῦντος." Ἑλληνικά, III, pp. 153 ff.

TARN, W. W.
"The Date of Milet I 3, No. 139." *Hermes*, 1930, pp. 446 ff.

VOGLIANO, A.
"Nuovi testi storici." *Riv. di Fil.*, 1926, pp. 320 ff.; 1927, pp. 501 ff.

WILHELM, A.
"Neue Beiträge zur griechischen Inschriftenkunde, Fünfter Teil." *Sitz. der wien. Akad.*, CCXIV, 4, 1932, pp. 16 ff.

INDEX

(This index does not include the names of magistrates in the tables, unless these also occur in the text. For list of tables see p. ix.)

Achaeans, crushed by Rome, 154 f.; proposed division of, 114; raided by Aetolians, 89; receive Delians, 86 f.; surrender to Antigonus Doson, 94
Achaia, Phthiotic, 111
Achaios, archon, 86 f., 146 n. 1
-adas, son of, Aetolian *agonothetes*, 111
Adeimantos, Delian *epimeletes*, 172
Aemilius, L., consul, 11 n. 1
Aetolians, accept Nikephoria, 119 n. 1; allies of Macedon, 89; aid of invoked by Athens, 144; and Amphictyonic Council, 120; and *asylia* of Teos, 130 n. 1; at peace with everybody, 115; found Soteria, 108 ff.; neutrality of, 123; preserve treaty with Athens, 98; protégés of Macedon, 131 n. 1; war of with Philip V, 111; wronged by Philip V, 121
Agamestor, philosopher, ends life, 11 n. 1
Agathokles, archon, 147 n. 1
Agathokles, regent of Egypt, 144
Agetas, Aetolian general, 123 n. 2
Agonothetae, Aetolian, 110 ff., 118
Aiantis, heads Tribal Cycle, 44 n. 1, 47, 62 ff., 64 n. 1, 78 ff., 174 ff.; undisturbed by Macedonian *phylae*, 80, 142 f.
Aigeis, Tribal Cycles resumed with, 47, 63 f.
Ainesidemos, of Sypalettos, 103 n. 1
Aischron, archon, 97

Aischron, son of Proxenos of Delphi, 100 f.
Alexander, of Epiros, 74 n. 1
Alexander of Kalydon, Aetolian general, 130 n. 1
Alexander, son of Krateros, 87
Alexandria, 132, 134, 136
Alexeas, Delphian archon, 123 n. 2
Alkibiades, archon, 26 n., 35 f.
Amein-, priest of Asklepios, 43
Ammonios, priest of Sarapis, 159 n. A
Amphictyonic Council, 120, 122, 126 n. 1
Amphictyons, Delian, Tribal Cycles of, 49; Delphian, 135 f., recognize *asylia* of Teos, 130 n. 1
Amphikrates, official of Delphian Pythais, 147 n. 1
Amynomachos, of Bate, heir of Epicurus, 35 n. 3
An-, priest of Asklepios, 60 n. 1
Anagrapheis, "registrars," 62, 69
Anarchia, of 88/7 B.C., 151, 160
Anaxandridas, Delphian archon, 119 and n. 2
Anaxikrates, archon in 279/8 B.C., 77 n. 1
Ankyle, 36 n. 7
Anthesterios, archon, 165 f., 168 f.
Antibios, *tamias*, 21, 38
Antigoneion tetrachmon, 37 f.
Antigonis, abolished, 140 ff., 141 n. 1; organized, 5 n. 1
Antigonos, Delian archon, 115
Antigonus, Doson, treaty of with Athens, 93 f.

188 INDEX

Antigonus, Gonatas, 35; appoints Athenian officials, 84 and n. 1, 85 and n. 1, 179 f.; captures Athens, 38, 65, 82: discharges Athenian officials, 21, 52; garrison of in Museum, 39, 31; government of in Athens, 88 n. 1; loses and regains Piraeus, 72 ff.; negótiates with Athens, 77 n. 1; treaties of, with Aetolians, 114, with Ptolemy II, 76, 131 n. 1; war of with Alexander, 87

Antigrapheis, 160 and n. 1

Antimachos, archon, 80 f., 83

Antioch in Persis, 129

Antiochos I, First Syrian War of, 73 n. 1

Antiochos II, 113, 125; concludes Second Syrian War, 131 n. 1

Antiochos III, accepts Leukophryena, 129, 131

Antiochos IV, and Popilius, 11 n. 1

Antipater, Macedonian regent, 47

Antiphilos, archon, 92 f.

Apellikon, expedition of to Delos, 147 n. 1

Aphrodite Hagne, priesthood of, 162 ff.

Aphrodite Stratonikis, 112 f., 124, 130

Apollo, Delian, priesthood of, 162, 170; Delphian, oracles of, 113, 124, 128

Apollodoros, Athenian general, 84 n. 1

Apollodoros, of Tanagra, Boeotian *hieromnemon*, 111

Apollonios, Egyptian *dioiketes*, 134

Apollonios, of Thria, Athenian general, 13, 15 n., 75 n. 1, 84 n. 1, 89, 180

Apollophanes, Magnesian *theoros*, 128 n. 1

Aratus, of Sicyon, agent of Ptolemy III, 93; attempt of on Piraeus, 89, 107; death of, 33 n. 7

Archelaos, archon, 36 n. 7

Archelaos, Delphian archon, 123 n. 2

Archestratos, priest of Asklepios, 60 n. 1

Archias, of Anaphlystos, Athenian general, 147 n. 1

Archikles, of Lakiadai, priest of Asklepios, 37

Archon, archon, 7, 180

Archon, herald of, 52 n. 1

Archon-names, significance of, 83 ff., 85 f., 177 f.

Archons, Delian, chronology of, 76 n. 1; senior, chosen κατὰ φυλάς, 52 ff., Tribal Cycles of, 50 ff., 94; undated, 34 n. A

Areopagites, as censors, 84 f.

Areopagus, commission of at Delos, 146 n. 1; growth in power of, 153 f. herald of, 52 n. 1

Areus, king of Sparta, 74 n. 1

Argeios, archonships of, 145, 147 n. 1, 151 f., 163 n.

Argos, 88, 108 n. 1

Aristagora, of Corinth, courtesan, 84 f.

Aristaichmos, archon, 169, 179

Aristion, of Pallene, *antigrapheus*, 160 n. 1

Aristogeiton, tyrannicide, 79

Aristomenes, first Delian gymnasiarch, 145 n. 1

Aristophanes, of Leukonoe, Athenian general, 13

Aristophon, archon, 36 n. 9, 180

Arrheneides, archon, 66, 76 n. 2, 85

Arsinoe, policy of, 73

Artemis, epiphany of, 128; Kalliste, Tribal Cycles of, 47 f., 64 n. 1

Asklepieion, 38 f., 40, 44 ff., 58, 61, 62 n. 1, 90, 94 n. 1, 97

Asklepios, cult-apparatus of listed separately, 42, 55; *ex-votos* of melted down and transferred to *tamiae*, 45 f., 61 f.; priests of, 300–

INDEX

276 B.C., 60 n. 1; *passim*. *See also* Tribal Cycles
Atene, 51 n. 2
Athamanes, recognize *asylia* of Teos, 130 n. 1
Athenagoras, of Melite, priest of Delian Artemis, 167 n. 2
Athenion, "tyrant" of Athens, 150 ff.
Athenodoros, archon, 89
Athenogenes, son of Tisarchos, of Halimus, priest of Zeus Kynthios, 159 n. B
Athens, accepts Leukophryena, 128 and notes; Antigonid administration of, 88 n. 1; constitutional changes in, 147 ff.; freed from Macedon, 90, 93; gifts of to Asklepios, 38 f.; gives privileges to Aiantis, 78 ff.; negotiates with Antigonus Gonatas, 76, 77 and n. 1; plays politics with archon-names, 81, 83 ff.; policy of, before Chremonidean War, 74, after 229 B.C., 93 f., during Social War, 97 ff., after 201 B.C., 140 ff.; recovers captives, 101; reformed by Rome, 152 f.; regains and loses Piraeus, 72 ff.; revolt of from Demetrius Poliorcetes, 70 f.
Attalis, created, 141 n. 1, 144
Attalos, I, and Athens, 144
Attalos II, 129
Auletes, 52 n. 1.
Autokles, of Oa, priest of Asklepios, 37

Babylon, 127
Babylos, Delphian archon, 123
Bendideia, 81 n. 1
Bendis, 81 and n. 1, 82
Berenike, daughter of Ptolemy II, 131 n. 1
Berenikidai, 95
Boeotians, accept Leukophryena, 128 n. 1; and Delphian Amphictyony, 111, 121 f.; arbitrate disputes with Athens, 89
Boiskos, of Phlya, priest of Asklepios, 37, 39, 40 f., 46 n. 2.

Calendar, Athenian, confusion of, 68, 92, 118, flexibility of cycles in, 5 and n. 1, 177; Ptolemaic, 132 ff.; Roman, confusion of, 11 n. 1
Cephallenia, 121
Chaeronea, battle of, 89
Chairephon, archon, 97 f.
Chalcis, 36 n. 8, 128 n. 1
Chalepos, of Naupaktos, Aetolian general, 123 n. 2
Charinos, priest of Asklepios, 55, 60 n. 1
Charisandros, of Halimus, *hoplomachos*, 105
Charixenos, Aetolian general, 108, 131; Delphian archon, 111
Charmikos, of Kikynna, priest of Zeus Kynthios, 169
Chase, G. H., 4 n. 1
Chios, and the Aetolian Soteria, 113 ff., 119 f., 131
Chremonidean War, 35, 38, 73 f., 76, 77 n. 1, 82, 103 n. 1
Cleruchy, founded at Delos, 86; dissolved, 173
Commissioners, of *Hiera* and Sacred Funds at Delos, 146 n. 1, 166 ff., 173
Corinth, 87
Council, Athenian, growth in prerogatives of, 148 ff., 150 ff., 153

Damokrates, Delphian archon, 110 ff., 118, 120 f.
Delos, cleruchy at dissolved, 173; corps of priests at, 167 n. 2; crisis in gymnasarchy at, 172 f.; date of organization of Athenian government in, 145 n. 1, 146 n. 1; financial year at, 146 n. 1; Pythais to from Athens, 147 n. 1

Delphi, and Smyrna, 126; Athenian archons at, 86; chronology of, 110 ff.; Pythais to from Athens, 147 n. 1; recognizes *asylia* of Teos, 130 n. 1; response of to Seleukos II, 113 f., 124; Soteria at, 108 ff.

Demagenes, priest of Asklepios, 60 n. 1

Demainetos, of Athmonon, Athenian envoy and general, 98 f.

Demetrias, abolished, 140 ff., 141 n. 1; organized, 5 n. 1

Demetrieian War, 107

Demetrios, grandson of Demetrius of Phaleron, 84 f.

Demetrios, son of Demetrius of Phaleron, 68 f.

Demetrius, of Phaleron, 5 n. 1, 68, 80

Demetrius Poliorcetes, honored by Athens, 143 n. 1; recalls Athenian exiles, 68 f.; revolt of Athens from, 47, 70

Demetrius II, appoints generals in Athens, 13, 15 n., 84 n. 1, 89, 179; marriage of with Stratonike, 131 n. 1; retains father's system in Athens, 88 n. 1; revolt of Athens at death of, 35 n. 3, 93, 96

Demochares, of Leukonoe, 74

Democracy, characteristics of, 178

Demokrates, of Kydathenaion, *antigrapheus*, 160

Demophilos, of Agryle, secretary for decrees, 160 n. 1

Demosioi, at Delos, 165 n. 1

Demosthenes, Athenian memories of, 74

De...tos, Aetolian *agonothetes*, 111

Dicastery, deprived of *euthyna* of magistrates, 148 ff.

Dikaiarchos, of Thria, commandant at Eretria, 15 n., 84 n. 1, 180

Dinsmoor, W. B., 4 n. 1, 13; work of on *Archons of Athens*, 3 ff.; bases of new Tribal Cycles of, 16, 19 f.; flexible calendar of, 5 and n. 1, 177;

Tribal Cycles of accepted in part, 7, 64 n. 1, 177, criticized, 46 n. 2, 89, 91 ff., 114, 115 n. 1, 139 f.; *et passim*

Diogenes, of Macedon, commandant at Athens, 88 and n. 1

Diognetos, archon, 115

Diokles, archon in 215/4 B.C., 20 f., 41 and n. 1, 44, 96 ff., 100 f.

Diokles, of Myrrhinus, priest of Asklepios, 58

Diomedon, 18 n. 1

Diomedon, archon, 16, 18 ff., 39 ff., 43 f., 46 n. 1, 75 and n. 1, 87 f., 93, 107, 114, 116, 139

Diomedon, son of Diokle-, 18 n. 1

Diomeia, 64 and n. 1, 143 n. 1

Dionysia and Demetrieia, in Athens, 108 n. 1; in Euboea, 108 n. 1

Dionysia and Seleukeia, at Erythrae, 108 n. 1

Dionysios, archon, 36 n. 9

Dionysios, of Lamptrai, Delian *hierokeryx*, 167 n. 2

Dionysos, Delian, priesthood of, 162, 170

Diophantos, of Hermos, commissioner of *Hiera* and Sacred Funds, 166

Diopheithes, priest of Asklepios, 60 n. 1

Dow, Sterling, 4 n. 1, 16 f., 35 n. 1, 60 n. 2, 66, 67 n. 1, 100, 117 n. 2

Ecclesia, loss by of legislative powers, 150 ff.

Echos, of Sunion, priest of Delian Asklepios, 167 n. 2

Egypt, Macedonian calendar in, 132 ff.

Eirenaios, priest of Sarapis, 159 n. A

Ekphantos, archon, 13, 15 n., 20, 75 n. 1, 84 n. 1, 93, 139, 180

Eleusinia, Great, 96 ff.

Eleusis, 15 n., 84 n. 1

Ephebes, listing of, 102 f.; officials of, 103 ff., 148; year of, 167 n. 1

INDEX

Ephialtes, of Sybridai, commissioner of *Hiera* and Sacred Funds, 166
Ephoros, of Ptelea, priest of Zeus Soter at Delos, 167 n. 2
Epicurus, philosopher, 35 n. 3, 72
Epikles, archon, 179
Epikrates, archon, 7, 145, 180
Epikrates, priest of Asklepios, 60 n. 1
Epimeletes, Delian, 151 n. 1, 164, 172
Era, Achaean, 154; Actian, 154
Eretria, 15 n., 87, 128 n. 1
Ergochares, archon, 91 ff., 94 f.
Ergokles, archon, 179
Erythrae, 108 n. 1
-es, Delphian archon, 121
Euainetos, archon, 45
Euandros, archon, 99 ff.
Euangelos, Delphian archon, 123 n. 2
Euboea, 108 n. 1
Eu- (Eubulos), archon, 44 f., 46, 55 f.
Eubulos, Magnesian *theoros*, 128 n. 1
Eubulos, of Marathon, priest of Delian Dionysos, 170
Eudidaktos, priest of Asklepios, 60 n. 1
[Eukr]ates (or [Epikr]ates), head of Delian Pythais, 147 n. 1
Euktemon, archon, 45 f.
Euktemon, of Melite, commissioner of *Hiera* and Sacred Funds, 173
Eumenes II, of Pergamum, 119 n. 1, 129
Eumenes, of Oinoe, priest of Delian Dionysos, 167 n. 2, 170
Eumnestos, priest of Asklepios, 60 n. 1
Eunikides, of Halai, priest of Asklepios, 58
Eunikos, of Sphettos, 103 n. 1
Eurykleides, of Kephisia, archon, 77 n. 1, 88, 89 n. 1, 114; death of, 36; friendliness of with Ptolemies, 94, 144; *tamias*, 87 f., 89 n. 1

Eustratos, of Oinoe, priest of Asklepios, 20 f.
Euthios, archon, 45 f.
Euthydemos, of Athmonon, commissioner of *Hiera* and Sacred Funds, 173
Euthykritos, archon, 45
Euxenippos, archon, 45
Exiles, restored by Demetrius Poliorcetes, 68 f.

Fêtes, how recognized, 130 n. 1
Finance, administration of, 94 n. 1

Gauls, 74 n. 1, 108
-goras, of Kropidai, priest of Hestia and Roma at Delos, 167 n. 2
Gorgias, archon, 35, 66, 74, 83
Gymnasiarchs, Delian, 145 ff., 164, 172 f., 176, 180

Hagnias, archon, 26 n., 35 n. 3
Hagnus, deme of secretary in 313/2 B.C., 64 n. 1
Harmodios, tyrannicide, 79
Hekate, 130 n. 1
Heliodoros, archon, 12 n. 1, 13, 94
Hellenotamiae, secretary of, 164
Heortios, son of Hermodoros, of Acharnai, *paidotribes*, 106 f.
Hepteteris, at Delos, 147 n. 1
Herakleitos, archon in 213/2 B.C., 90, 103 n. 1
Herakleitos, archon in 96/5 B.C., 147 and n. 1
Herakleitos, of Athmonon, 87 f.
Herias, Delphian *hieromnemon*, 111
Hermias, archon, 36 n. 9, 179
Hermodoros, I, son of Heortios, of Acharnai, *paidotribes*, 106; II (his grandson), *paidotribes*, 107
Herys, Delphian archon, 111
Hieromnemones, Aetolian, 109 ff., 120 ff.; Boeotian, 111, 122; Delphian, 110 f.; Phthiotic, 121

INDEX

Hieron, archon, 19, 81 n. 1, 107 f., 114, 136
Hierophantes, archon, 86
Hipparchs, appointed by Antigonus Gonatas, 84 f.
Hybrias, Delphian archon, 123 n. 2
Iacchus, 152
Ios, 113 ff., 129 n. 3
-ippos, of Erikeia, son of, commissioner of *Hiera* and Sacred Funds, 167 f.
Isigenes, archon, 76 n. 1

Jason, archon, in *ca.* 233 B.C., 35
Jason, archon in 109/8 B.C., 169 n. 1

Kallaischros, archon, 84 n. 1
Kalliades, of Aigilia, priest of Asklepios, 21, 115
Kallias, Aetolian *agonothetes*, 111
Kallias, of Gargettos, commissioner of *Hiera* and Sacred Funds, 166
Kallikles, of Prospalta, son of, commissioner of *Hiera* and Sacred Funds, 167 f
Kallimachos, of Aphidna, polemarch, 79
Kallistratos, archon, 36, n. 6
Kallistratos II, archon, 166
Kassander, 69
Katapaltaphetes, 107
Kekropis, heads Tribal Cycle, 63
Kellog, O. D., 5 n. 1
Kerameikos, meeting place of Ecclesia, 152
Kimon, archon in 289/8 B.C., 69 ff.
Kimon, archon in 237/6 B.C., 12 n. 1, 13, 84 n. 1
Kleigenes, of Halai?, secretary, 45
Kleomachos, archon, 81, 83
Kleomenes, of Sparta, 94
Koroibos, archon, 35
Kosmetes, made responsible to Council, 148 ff.
Kriton, of Marathon, secretary for decrees, 160 n. 1

Ktesippos, of Anakaia, priest of Sarapis, 164
Ktesonides, priest of Asklepios, 37 f.
Kydenor, archon, 35, 68, 114, 118 n. 1
Kypaira, 111, 120 f.

Lachares, "tyrant," 3, 61, 70
Lailianos, archon, 76 n. 1
Lamia, 89
Lamptrai, deme of secretary in *ca.* 318/7 B.C., 64 n. 1
Lebadea, 110
-leides, of Oion, secretary of the Council and *demos*, 160 n. 1
Leon, priest of Sarapis, 159 n. A
Leonides, of Phlya, priest of Asklepios, 179
Leontis, heads Tribal Cycle, 63
Leukophryena, history of foundation of, 36 n. 8, 124, 128 ff.; proclamation at in 192/1 B.C., 126 n. 1
Licinius, C., consul, 11 n. 1
L . . on, son of Miltiades, of Alopeke, secretary, 66
Lykeas, archon, 26 n., 35 n. 3
Lykeas, of Rhamnus, priest of Asklepios, 21, 38
Lykomedes, Magnesian *theoros*, 128 n. 1
Lykomedes, of Konthyle, priest of Asklepios, 37
Lykophron, of Sunion, priest of Zeus Kynthios, 169
L . . . . . os, Delphian *hieromnemon*, 110 f.
Lysanias, of Melite, priest of Asklepios, 21
Lysiades, archon, 115 and n. 1
Lysias, archon, 13, 66 f.
Lysias, of Diomeia, secretary, 143
Lysias, priest of Asklepios, 60 n. 1
Lysikles, of Sypalettos, priest of Asklepios, 41 f., 43, 46, 106

INDEX

Lysitheides, archon, 81 n. 1
Lyttos, 86

M-, of Kolonos, priest of Asklepios, 59 and n. 1, 60 and n. 1
Macedonian War, First, 111, 121, 136
Magnesia, military colonists at, 127
Magnesians, found and announce Leukophryena, 36 n. 8, 128 ff.; use Athenian archon for chronological purposes, 86
Mantias, Delphian archon, 123
Marathon, deme of official of Zeus Kynthios, 169 n. 1
Medeios, of Piraeus, dictatorship of, 145, 151 and n. 1, 152
Megartas, Delphian archon, 121 ff., 130 n. 1
Menekrates, archon, 92, 103 n. 1
Menekrates, of Lebedea, 110 f.
Menon, 21
Meritt, B. D., 4 n. 1
Meton, astronomer, 3
Metonic Cycle, 5 and n, 1, 75, 78 n. 1, 92, 118, 162, 175 n. 2
Metrophanes, archon, 145, 173, 180
Mikion, archon, 179
Mikion, of Kephisia, collaborates with brother, 94, 144; death of, 36 n. 7
Mikion, of Semachidai, priest of Zeus Kynthios, 167 n. 2, 169
Mithradates, of Pontus, 152
Mithres, friend of Epicurus, 72
Mnasilochos, archon, 76 n. 1
Moiragoras, Magnesian *stephanephoros*, 128 n. 2
Museum, Macedonian garrison in, 39, 81, 115

Naupaktos, Peace of, 101
Neanthes, of Cyzicus, 79
Nemea and Heraia, at Argos, 108 n. 1
Nikandros, son of, of Ankyle, ephebe official, 105

Nikephoria, 119 n. 1
Niketes, archon, 92
Nikias, archon in 296/5 B.C., 60 n. 1, 69 f.
Nikias, archon in 124/3 B.C., 76 n. 1
Nikias, of Otryne, archon, 52 n. 1
Nikodamos, Delphian archon, 119 n. 2
Nikomachos, archon, 179
Nikomachos, priest of Asklepios, 21
Nikonides, of Phlya, priest of Asklepios, 59, 60 n. 1
Nock, A. D., 4 n. 1
Notopoulos, James, 78 n. 2
Noumenios, of Phyle, priest of Anios, 167 n. 2
Nymphodoros, of Marathon, Delian kleiduchos, 167 n. 2
Nymphs, Sphragitic, 79

Odeum, burned, 86
Oinophilos, of Paionidai, polemarch, 53
Olbios, archon, 35 f.
Olympiodoros, archon, "dictatorship" of, 62, 69; general, 72, 74
Olympiodoros, of Pallene, Delian *mantis*, 167 n. 2
Onetor, of Melite, priest of Asklepios, 40, 54 ff., 60 n. 1
-onides, son of Androkles, ephebe official, 105
Orgeones, of Bendis, 81 and n. 1, 82
-os, son of Lykos, of Alopeke, secretary, 67

P- (Polystratos?), archon, 42 and n. 1, 43, 45, 47, 56, 115 f.
Paiania, unequal size of Upper and Lower, 12 n. 1; Lower, 75
Paidotribate, hereditary office, 106 f.
Pairisades, 135 n. 1
Panakton, 15 n.
Panathenaia, Great, 35 n. 3, 135 n. 1
Pantias (Pantiades), archon, 36 n. 6
Paredri, of archons, 52 n. 1

194 INDEX

Patroklos, Ptolemaic admiral, 74 n. 1
Peace, of 261 B.C., 76, 77 and n. 1; of 255 B.C., 115, 131 n. 1; of Naupaktos, 101; of Seleukos II and Ptolemy III, 126
Peithidemos, archon, 43, 73 f.
Peloponnesus, 128 n. 1
Pelops, archon, 20, 86 f., 139 f., 146 n. 1
Perigenes, of Eupyridai, Delian *auletes*, 167 n. 2
Perseus, capture of, 11 n. 1
Ph-, priest of Asklepios, 45, 60 n. 1
Phaidrias, archon, 169 n. 2, 170
Phaidrippos, priest of Asklepios, 60 n. 1
Phaidros, of Sphettos, 69 ff., 103 n. 1
Phanomachos, priest of Asklepios, 60 n. 1
Phanostratos, archon, 81, 83
Pharsalos, 121
Pheidostratos, archon, 80 f., 83
Philadelphia, 134
Philaitolos, Delphian archon, 121 ff.
Phileas, of Eitea, priest of Asklepios, 21, 115
Philip V, accepts Leukophryena, 36 n. 8, 128 n. 1; and Phthiotic Achaia, 111, 120 f.; preserves peace with Athens, 98; rupture with Athens, 140 ff.
Philippos, archon, 66 ff.
Philippos, of Ionidai, priest of Asklepios, 38
Philippos, priest of Asklepios, 55, 57, 60 n. 1
Philochares, of Oa, priest of Asklepios, 40, 54 f., 57, 59, 60 n. 1
Philokrates, of Hamaxanteia, priest of Sarapis, 164 ff., 167 n. 2, 168
Philokrates, of Hekale, priest of Asklepios, 37 f.
Philokrates, son of Philokrates, priest of Sarapis twice, 151 n. 2
Philoktemon, priest of Asklepios, 60 n. 1

Philon, philosopher, 179
Philoneos, archon, 12 n. 1, 26 n., 102 ff., 105 ff.
Philopappos, *agonothetes*, 79, archon, 76 n. 1
Philostratos, archon, 81, 83
Phocis, 128 n. 1
Phoryskides, of Daidalidai (Leukonoe, Halimus?), 18, 36 n. 4, 88
Phthiotis (Tetras and Achaia), 121
Phylae, epoch of eleven, 141 n. 1, 143; *passim*.
Phyle, 15 n.
Phyleus, of Eleusis, 19, 21 n. 1, 44, 54, 59 f., 60 n. 1
Piraeus, attacked by Aratus, 89; heap of ruins, 86; regained and lost by Athens, 72 ff., 83; seat of Macedonian commandant, 88 n. 1; separate from Athens, 82 f.
Pistoklees, of Anaphlystos, *antigrapheus*, 160 n. 1
Pleistainos, archon, 172, 179; cf. 139
Pnyx, deserted by *demos*, 151
Popilius, 11 n. 1
Polyeuktos, archon, 19, 85, 90 n. 1, 107 ff., 112, 114, 117 f., 120, 123, 128, 129 n. 3, 131, 133
Polyeuktos, of Bate, 35 n. 3
Polykleitos, Delphian archon, 123
Polystratos, archon, 81 ff. *See* P-
Polyxenos, priest of Asklepios, 58
Praetor, Roman, in Macedon, 153, 155
Praochos, Delphian archon, 112
Praxiteles, of Eiresidai, priest of Asklepios, 37 f.
Prokles, of Piraeus, priest of Asklepios, 37
Pronapes, of Prospalta, secretary of Council and *demos*, 160 n. 1
Pronni, 121
Protagoras, of Pergase, priest of Asklepios, 20
Ptolemais, and archon-cycle, 53 f., 53 n. 1; and priestly and secre-

tary-cycle, 95 f.; creation of, 91 ff.; heads Tribal Cycles, 142 f., 145; undisturbed, by abolition of Macedonian *phylae*, 143, by creation of Attalis, 144

Ptolemy II, intervenes in Greece, 73; peace of, with Antigonus Gonatas, 76, 131 n. 1, with Antiochos II, 131 n. 1

Ptolemy III, calendar of Egypt under, 132, 134 ff.; enmity of with Aetolians, 114; finances Aratus, 93, Kleomenes, 94; operations of in Third Syrian War, 126 f.; relations of with Athens, 94 f.

Ptolemy IV, calendar of Egypt under, 133 ff.

Ptolemy V, honored by Athens, 143 f.

Ptolemy VI, peace of with Antiochos IV, 11 n. 1

Pydna, date of battle of, 11 n. 1

Pylades, of Perithoidai, priest of Delian Artemis, 169 n. 2

Pyrrhus, of Epirus, 73

Pythais, Delian, 147 n. 1; Delphian, 147 n. 1

Pytharatos, archon, 43

Pythia, announcement of, 131; proclamations at, 126 and n. 1; relation of to Soteria, 108 ff., 118

Pythonikos, priest of Asklepios, 60 n. 1

Rhamnus, 13, 15 n., 180; deme of secretary in 308/7 B.C., 64 n. 1

Rhodes, aid of asked for by Athens, 144

Robert, L., 125

Romans, complaints of Achaeans to, 87; give Delos to Athens, 146; recognize *asylia* of Teos, 130 n. 1; remodel institutions of Athens, 150 ff.

-s, of Kettos, polemarch, 53

-s, of Oion, priest of Delian Apollo, 167 n. 2

Salamis, 15 n.; officers of *thiasos* at, 90 n. 1; relation of to Aiantis, 79 f.; *thiasos* of Bendis at, 81 n. 1

Sarapieion, 165 n. 1

Sarapion, 79

Sarapion, priest of Sarapis, 159 n. A

Sarapion, of Melite, *agonothetes*, 151 n. 1, head of Delphian Pythais, 147 n. 1

Secretaries, undated, 34 notes

Secretary, for decrees, 160 n. 1; of the Council, 160 n. 1; of the Council and *demos*, 160 n. 1; cf. 100 n. 1; of the *demos*, 76 n. 2, 160 n. 1

Seleukis, 125, 127

Seleukos II, accepts Soteria, 136; crosses Tauros Mts., 127; requests *asylia* for Smyrna and shrine of Aphrodite Stratonikis, 113 f., 124 ff., 130

Seleukos, of Acharnai, priest of Aphrodite Hagne, 163 n.

Seleukos, of Pergase, priest of the Great Gods at Delos, 167 n. 2, 168

Senate, of Rome, procrastinates, 153

-sides, of Alopeke, priest of Asklepios, 21, 46 n. 2

Smikythos, of Anagyrus, priest of Asklepios, 37

Smyrna, accessible to Aetolians, 115; decree of identified, 112 ff.; negotiations of with Delphi and Seleukos II, 124 ff., 130 f.

Social War, 99, 101, 111, 123

Sosistratos, archon, 77 n. 1, 81, 83, 103 n. 1

Soteria, announced in Egypt, 132 ff.

Soteria, Aetolian, penteteric, 109 f., 131; records of, 111 f.; trieteric?, 119 f.; time of year of, 108; when accepted by Athens, 114, by Smyrna, 131; when founded, 108, 136

Soteria, annual, 110, 119, 135 and n. 1, 136

Sotion, son of Kleon, of Delphi, death of, 132 ff.
Sparta, ally of Athens, 73; at war with Aetolians, 114
Spartokos, 155 n. 1
Strategia, filled by joint action of king and *demos*, 84 f.; for districts of Attica, 14 f., 88 n. 1; for the mercenaries?, 70; for the navy, 147 n. 1
Stratios of Phegaia, *antigrapheus*, 160
Stratoniceia, 130 n. 1
Stratonike, sister of Antiochos II, 131 n. 1
Stratonike, Thea, cult of as Aphrodite Stratonikis, 113, 124 ff.; death of, 130
Sulla, 7, 86, 139; restores Roman system in Athens, 150 ff.
Sunion, 15 n.; deme of priest of Asklepios, 37
Syria, 126
Syrian War, First, 73; Second, 115, 131 n. 1; Third, 125 ff.

Tamiae, of Athena, 44 f., 61, 62 n. 1, 63; secretary-cycle of, 65 f.
Tauros Mts., 126 f.
Telesias, of Phlya, priest of Asklepios, 58
Tenos, 113 ff.
Teos, 129 n. 3; *asylia* of, 130 n. 1
Theaitetos, archon, 180
Thebes, Phthiotic, 120
Theo-, priest of Asklepios, 60 n. 1
Theobios, of Acharnai, priest, 163 n.
Theodoros, of Marathon, commissioner of *Hiera* and Sacred Funds, 166
Theodoros, of Melite, priest of Asklepios, 37
Theodotos, *agoraestes*, 132 f., 135
Theokles, archon, 147 and n. 1
Theophemos, archon, 114
Theophilos, archon, 12 n. 1

Theopompos, archon, 76 n. 1
Theorodoki, 136
Thersilochos, archon, 89
Thersippos, of Acharnai, 64 n. 1
Thersippos, son of Thrasippos, of Acharnai, 102
Thesmothetae, appointed by Antigonus Gonatas, 85; secretary of, 52 n. 1; tribal distribution of, 52 f.
Thompson, Homer, 117 n. 2
Thracians, devotees of Bendis in Athens and Piraeus, 81 and n. 1, 82 f.
Thrason, of Anakaia, 77 n. 1
Thrasybulos, priest of Asklepios, 55, 60 n. 1
Thrasynon Delian archon, 75
Thrasyphon, archon, 7, 12 and n. 1, 75 and n. 1, 95 f.
Thymochares, of Sphettos, *agonothetes*, 73 archon, 26 n., 103 and n. 1, 106 f.
Tigris, river, 127, 129 n. 2
Timarchides, archon, 179
Timarchos, archon, 20, 139
Timokles, of Eiresidai, priest of Asklepios, 48
Timokles, of Halai, priest of Asklepios, 99, 102
Tralles, 129
Treasurer, of Military Funds, 94 n. 1
Tribal Cycles, 321-307 B.C., 47 n. 1; 263-256 B.C., 80; beginning with Aiantis, 62 ff., 174 ff.; of Dinsmoor, 7, 16 ff., 19 f., 46 n. 2, 49 n. 1, 64 n. 1, 89, 91 ff., 97 f., 99 ff., 110, 114, 115 n. 1, 133 f., 139 f., 145 n. 1, 146 n. 1, 147, 155, 168, 177; limits of records, 6, 44, 61, 90 f., 155; not used for elective offices, 160 n. 1; stability of, 65 f.; synchronized in 109 B.C., 175 n. 2; two forms of, 6, 48 ff.; of priests: of Anios, 139, of Artemis at Delos, 169 and n. 2, of Artemis Kal-

liste, 48, 64 n. 1, of Asklepios, 48, 140, 171 ff., *et passim*, of Great Gods, 48, 168, of Sarapis, 48, 165, *et passim*, of Zeus Kynthios, 168 f.; of prytany-secretaries, 48, *et passim*, and their subordinates, 160 n. 1; of secretaries of the Hellenotamiae, 48; of secretaries of *tamiae* of Athena, 48

Tribal Cycles in allotted order, 48 ff.; of archons, 50 ff.; of priests: of Aphrodite Hagne, 49, 162 ff., of Apollo at Delos, 162, 170, of Asklepios, 49, 54 ff., 59 f., 174 ff., of Dionysos at Delos, 162, 170, of Great Gods, 168, of Roma at Delos, 162, 170, of Sarapis, 164 ff., of Zeus Kynthios, 169; of prytanies, 49, 53 n. 1, 147; of prytany-secretaries, 49, 145 ff.; of secretaries of *tamiae*, 49 and n. 1

Tribal distribution, of officials, 143, 170 f.
Tychandros, archon, 145
Typos, defined, 21 n. 2

Xennias, Aetolian *agonothetes*, 111
Xenokles, archon, 7, 11 n. 1, 20, 140, 146 n. 1
Xenokritos, of Aphidna, priest of Asklepios, 37, 46 and n. 2, 47, 56
Xenon, archon, 179
Xenophon, archon, 71, 77 n. 1
Xypete, deme of priest of Asklepios, 115 and n. 1

Zenodotos, Magnesian *stephanephoros*, 128 n. 2
Zenon, agent of Apollonios, 134
Zenon, philosopher, 77 n. 1
Zoilos, of Phlya, priest of Asklepios, 20

INDEX OF INSCRIPTIONS

IG² II 477: 77 n. 1
IG² II 670: 35
IG² II 682: 69 ff.
IG² II 702: 66
IG² II 703: 66 ff.
IG² II 704: 77 n. 1
IG² II 773: 35 n. 1
IG² II 783: 102
IG² II 791: 16 ff., 87 f.
IG² II 796/7: 67 f.
IG² II 845 and 652: 99 ff.
IG² II 1534: 21 ff., 37 f., 39 f., 44 ff., 59 n. 1, 115 ff.

IG² II 1706: 50 ff., 90, 96 f.
IG² II 2336: 50 ff., 147

BCH, 1908, p. 438, no. 64: 167 n. 2
BCH, 1930, p. 269: 179
Ditt., *Syll.*³, 402: 109, 119; 557: 128 n. 2
Fouilles de Delphes, III 1, no. 483: 112 ff., 124 ff.
Fouilles de Delphes, III 2, nos. 48, 49: 147 n. 1
Inschr. von Magnesia, no. 37: 36, 95
Inschr. von Magnesia, no. 91: 135 n. 1